From Our Contrib

Participating in this book pro_____ ___ ___ _..y me. It gave legitimacy to the Tree Story I had not shared and to the feelings I had not acknowledged. I "came out of the closet" with my joy in communicating with trees and discovered I was not alone. Thank you, Shiila, for inviting me to write my story.

Lynne Russell, author

It was wonderful to write up my experience with the Tree of Light. This is a part of my life I never want to forget, that I want to share, and one that has greatly enhanced my spiritual growth. I hope you, too, will realize that Grace can happen and happen BIG! Love and Light!

Joy Pendleton, author

The moment I heard about *Intimacy with Trees* I felt a great sense of connection and thought, "I want to know more!" How much better can it get than people from all walks of life, coming together to celebrate their stories of nature and the friendship and wisdom offered from trees. I want to be a part of it!

Holly Melear, author and artist

It was such a pleasure to think about my relationship with trees for the *Intimacy with Trees* project. I have been climbing trees and sitting on their branches since I was a toddler. I still do it on occasion, which makes more than fifty years of intimacy with trees, and it still feels like climbing into my mother's arms.

Carol Flake Chapman, poet

My last name is Elms so it seems quite natural to be inspired by these amazing stories. My illustrations invoke the impressions that linger in my dreams after reading these passages of spirit and wonder of the nature that surrounds and towers over us.

Cheryl Elms, artist

Compiled by Shiila Safer

Edited by Sharon Carter

Intimacy
with
TREES

2nd Tier Publishing

Published by:
2nd Tier Publishing
13501 Ranch Road 12, Ste 103
Wimberley, TX 78676

ISBN 978-0-9894642-4-6

Book design by Dan Gauthier
Cover art by Sharon Carter

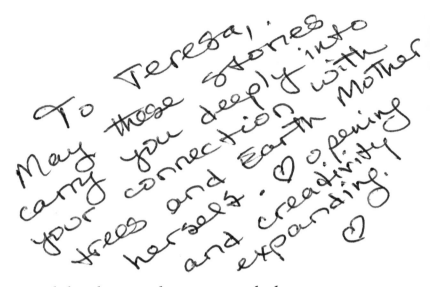

To Teresa,
May these stories
carry you deeply into
your connection with Mother
trees and Earth Mother
herself. ♡ opening
and creativity
expanding.
♡

To our beloved trees and to everyone who loves you.

To our beloved Mother Earth and to everyone who loves you.

To All Our Relations and our co-creation with you.

To humans returning to the Web of Life.

With love,
Sheila Sophia

Table of Contents

Acknowledgments

by Shiila Safer

First, I give thanks to the trees. Thank you for your wisdom and your guidance every step of the way!

Next, I'd like to express my heartfelt gratitude to all 52 contributing writers and artists for your stories, poems, messages, meditations and illustrations. We are all co-creators with the trees! It makes me so happy to know that writers from Australia, Italy, Tasmania, and throughout the United States participated in this grand experiment in global collaboration. Thank you for sharing your hearts and your special trees with us all!

There are so many people whose good energy helped birth this book over the past few years! We give special thanks to our editor extraordinaire, Sharon Carter—without your skilled eye for editing, your patience and art direction, this beautiful book would not be what it is today! We also thank Sharon for the cover art, which captures the essence of the book so beautifully. Another key player is Cheryl Elms, talented illustrator of many stories—we thank you! Dan Gauthier and 2nd Tier Publishing, thank you for your generous labor of love—book design, typesetting and layout which expresses the heart of the stories so gracefully. Thanks to Karen Smith for your eagle-eye proofing under a short deadline.

We appreciate the generosity of all the artists who offered rewards for our Kickstarter fundraiser campaign—Faith Harrison, Joy Phoenix, Cheryl Elms, and Sharon Carter—thank you! Thanks to Roger McBee for your art direction and Dan Gauthier for the filming of the video. What patience you both had! BIG appreciation to Dane Hurt, videographer, for giving us a helping hand when we really needed it, and creating a great video for our Kickstarter campaign!

A HUGE thank you to Will Taegel and Judith Yost, and to all of our contributors to our fundraising campaign—you made publication of the book possible! We are so heartened by you all!

Many thanks beyond words go to Dan Gauthier, my beloved husband and business partner, for sharing the vision for *Intimacy with Trees* from the very beginning, and seeing it all the way through to the end!

Much gratitude to all of you (you know who you are) who held my hand, kept the faith, reminded me about divine timing and lovingly supported me and the book through this birthing process!

Preface

by Will Taegel

As you hold this book in your hands, I invite you into a brief meditation. Return to a childhood scene or, if you like, a more recent time. As you journey into the mists of consciousness and the web of fields, allow a tree to come to your mind's eye. Approach the tree as you would an old friend, one that you may not have seen in some time. Out of respect ask the tree if you can come closer and touch its bark. If you gain permission, run your hands over the bark and feel the texture.

Then, sit down at the base of the trunk and recall moments that the tree assisted you. Note that this tree has an interest in your well being and in your evolution as a person. See if the tree has something to say about the forests of Earth. As you sit, be aware that trees are the largest plants on Earth. They are complex and share much of our DNA. Since your tree harnesses energy from the Sun, it can send its packets of photons through your body/mind/soul, even as it did so long ago. Take a breath and breathe the light through yourself and send it to a place of need in your life. As you breathe, be aware that an average tree can provide enough oxygen each day for four people. There is more than enough for you on this day.

Pause. Give thanks for all of the trees across our planet who toil, mostly thankless, on our behalf. Look and see if your tree meets you in late summer or fall. Look around on the ground. Are there seeds lying on the soil around you? If so, touch the seed and notice the soft tissue that holds the basis of a new tree, of new life. That seed holds the possibility of a mature tree-in-the-making. Look inside and see that within you is possibility. There is within you the seed of what our Creator intends for you to be. Even as there is a strong oak within the seed of an oak tree, so there is a possible you unfolding, being pulled by your sitting with your friend the tree.

Return to the trunk in the laser light of your awareness. The trunk of this tree supports the crown of branches and leaves. It transports food from the leaves and needles to all living parts of your tree. Breathe in these bountiful resources for your own growth, provided by our Creator.

Beneath the inner bark is a thin layer called the cambium that each year develops new cells of inner bark on its outer wall and new sapwood cells on its inner wall. Listen to your tree. As it grows, old inner layers of sapwood die and become heartwood, a rigid fiber that gives the tree its strength. As you meditate and allow your shoulders to slide down your back into a restful mode, know that this experienced tree is there for you. There for you all of this time. There for you to build up your heart, the fiber of your being. Together, you can become the heartwood of larger Earth.

Now, come back to this marvelous book—*Intimacy with Trees*, the one you hold in your hands. The book was compiled not only to assist with increasing your intimacy with trees but to encourage humans to return to the natural order. In order to make this return possible, we need to develop a working knowledge of the mother tongue spoken by all creation. Yes. Including us humans. Likely, you share with me a forgetting of this mother tongue. Yet, as I absorb the bursts of creativity in these pages, I resonate and find my base vocabulary underneath usual language being strengthened.

Stories of creation, poetry of seeing, and artful illustrations reach out to me, tugging me along, though sometimes I am reluctant. Within my inner council I have sub-selves that have been reared by our mainstream culture. You know that culture. The one that would label this book as being for tree huggers. But, soon, as I read on, those aspects within quieten and make room for a deeper hearing. With Larry Winters I am called to lay my head in the lap of a mother tree. With Shiila Safer, the guiding spirit behind our book, I learn to rekindle my trust in trees and ask them to trust me. I am invited for us to form a partnership of trust. This partnership is no easy task, given how we humans have treated our tall sisters and brothers.

With Oberto Airaudi, "Falco," the founder of Damanhur, I am further invited into a new covenant emerging between humans and trees. Dare I hope? And can this emerging agreement provide the basis for souls to link with stars? And, as I move through our book, I find not only poetry, stories, and art. Specific practical projects reach out and offer encouragement. Projects like those described by Wendy Grace and her tree friends at Hawks Hill in Northern California. Projects like those hinted at in various Earthtribers' contributions. And songs. Don't forget the songs of trees. I turn to a page with Wynn Renee Freeland's song and embrace not only the words but the music—"I've searched the world over, and come back to you…"

I hold the *Intimacy with Trees* book in my hand, running my palms across the pages. I open to a poem. I push the middle of the book down to hold it in place. I recall that somewhere I read that it takes one tree to produce 62 books. Some tree out there, somewhere, has given its life so I can hold and read. I pause and give thanks for the sacrifices made by living creatures all around, especially for the trees who make possible so much in my life. I likely will order the electronic version as well, so I can refer to its life force in the form of words, carrying it with me. I take comfort in that avenue of reading. But with certain books I want to hold them in my hands. In doing so, I acknowledge the tree not only for the paper but for going with me every step of my Earth walk, for being patient with my lack of awareness, and for teaching me a forgotten language of intimacy.

           Will Taegel, Spring, 2015

Introduction

by Shiila Safer

It is with great joy that I write these words of introduction to *Intimacy with Trees*. My heart is full of gratitude for all of the storytellers, artists, and poets who so generously shared their experiences with us. To quote one of my teachers, Dr. Will Taegel, "It's in the sharing of our stories that our world grows." These stories and illustrations emerged from the world-wide community with the power of an exhilarating waterfall cascading over a rock ledge, bringing us its tremendous energy. When we put out the call for people to share their stories about special trees, the response was almost overwhelming! We struck a chord that resonated deeply among others.

We are honored to present narratives about people and trees, which will open hearts, and draw us into a deeper intimacy with ourselves, as well as with the other forms of life on Earth. These stories are as varied as the trees they describe, yet there are common threads that run through all: people and trees are capable of direct communication; there is tree wisdom available to those who listen and observe; and children have an innate understanding and affinity for trees.

Recently, a gift came to me in an unexpected way. I was in the park with my eighteen-month old grandson. He reached down to the ground and picked up a handful of dried oak leaves and gleefully ran to the nearest oak tree and touched the leaves in his hand to the bark of the tree, calling, "Tree! Tree"! Then he turned and ran to the next tree, doing the same thing. After that, he discovered a tree stump low to the ground, and ran to it. He stuffed the leaves down the hole in the center of the stump, then climbed up and stood happily on the stump, looking for the next tree. This went on for about twenty minutes, as we made our way through the park, me following some distance behind.

I was deeply moved to see my grandson's innate knowledge that the leaves belonged to the tree, and to witness his joyful, natural connection with them. Clearly, a delightful exchange between this little boy and the trees was taking place. For many of us, memorable relationships with trees began at early ages, such as this, and remained a constant throughout our lives.

This has been true for me. As long as I can remember, I have recognized trees as friends, protectors, confidants, teachers, and guides. When the notion of collecting stories of peoples' most intimate moments with trees popped into my head, I immediately climbed up into a 200-year-old Live Oak that I call Grandmother, and I felt a wave of encouragement. The organic unfolding and expansion of *Intimacy with Trees* from a tiny seed of an idea, to a full-grown life of its own, is tangible proof of the support I felt. I am both humbled and honored to participate in this co-creation with brothers and sisters and trees from around the world.

At this point in time, the scales are tipping precariously out of balance between mankind and a healthy planet, so it is especially important for us to seek guidance and wisdom from the Earth. This takes shifting our paradigm from the failed attempt of human domination and control to building a new relationship based on mutual respect, and living in collaboration with all creation. How will we do this?

The "more-than-humans," a term introduced by David Abram in *The Spell of the Sensuous* (1996), refers to the non-human forms of life on Earth: trees, wind, winged-ones, four-leggeds, rocks, plants, etc. They offer mankind a wealth of resources. If and when we open ourselves to respectfully experience them, they offer support, nurturing, guidance, wisdom, and a possibility for humanity to learn how to live in harmonious balance on this beautiful blue planet.

In Will Taegel's book, *The Mother Tongue: Intimacy in the Eco-field* (2012), Will invites us to access a language that exists underneath all languages; an ability we all have, to communicate with the "more-than-human" world and the eco-fields, or energy fields that come through the specific ecology of the landscape we are in. He takes us on a journey that leads us to a deeper realm beneath our words, language, and beliefs. We set out on an exploration into the language of nature, "the Mother Tongue." Opening to its secrets, can we tap into the vast intelligence that surrounds us all the time?

As our vision unfolds for *Intimacy with Trees*, we see the possibility of a "more-than-human" book series, with *Intimacy with Trees* introducing the rest. The premise of the series is that we all have the ability to communicate with the "more-than-human" world and with our environment in an intimate way, and that many of us have already experienced communication with "more-than-humans." The series would provide a container and an outlet for our collective stories to emerge. As you read this book, think back to your childhood and see what memories come alive inside of you.

In the evolution of this book, visible stories made it onto pages, and internal stories took place in the lives of authors as they recalled their tale with a significant tree. We are so grateful to hear about the depth of discovery and intimacy which has been shared regarding the memories and experiences behind the scenes, as well as the candid stories you are about to read. These experiences are at the heart of *Intimacy with Trees*. They provide the heartbeat you feel pulsing behind the words.

As you will see from the depth and breadth of the stories being told, messages of wisdom come through in a variety of ways. Some of us feel them, others hear them, see them, or sense them. However you receive your messages, it takes practice to communicate. Learning to trust what you receive comes over time. Perhaps reading these stories will assist you in your own relationship with the natural world.

Imagine a ladder leaning against a large oak tree. At the top is a tree house beckoning to you. As you climb the ladder one rung at a time, feel the deep peace of the tree engulf you. Find a comfortable spot in our tree house and settle in for story time. Or, if a tree calls you to spread out a blanket and sit at its base to read, settle down and let these stories, poems and meditations seep deeply into your wellbeing. Let them inspire you and guide you into your own intimate moments with trees. Beyond that, these stories can be a doorway into another realm. We invite you to walk through the doorway into a more profound connection with the natural world.

Stories and Poetry

The leaf of every tree brings a message from the unseen world. Look, every falling leaf is a blessing.

Rumi

A Creation Story

by R.Maya Briel

illustrated by Karina Konupek

In a Vision Quest with the Earthtribe, spring of 2012, we gathered to bring our conscious efforts and awareness to the earth, and connect with nature. We had many Questers who had been in deep preparation all year, and many others in supporting roles. I was within the encampment, holding an "intent" for my friend who had put a "stake of intent" into the ground the previous year. At the same time that my friend (now known as Clear Tree) was gifted her vision, Star Heart was leading us in a nightly mediation of awareness and healing. My experience of being breathed by the Sacred Pipe happened while Clear Tree was being breathed by the Tree. This story is part of what came through.

Creation began in the heavens with the beautiful, full and wise creator being we call "Earth." Earth's nature was very deep and passionate with fire. She was continuously harmonizing and seeking to balance herself. Looking outside of herself, she spotted a passing comet full of frozen water just perfect for her fire. Fire and water came together in a primal dance to form the steamy air that brought more creation. Earth learned much from her elemental friends, but still she yearned for a deeper, more intimate connection. So she opened once more to the universe, and called out for a partner.

She was heard by a vast creative being we now call Nature. As Earth and Nature came together, new levels of creating, harmonizing, and balancing brought abundant life. The abundance began impacting and catching the awareness of the Star People from the Milky Way. These Star People wanted to experience and learn from these creator beings so they danced their spirits to "Earth and Nature" and were born from Earth.

They came as a wave called Humanity. Humanity thrived and grew and developed at the feet of Mother Earth, who nurtured and supported and freely shared her abundance. As children, Humanity was into everything: building, exploring, conquering, and learning to control their world. Humanity forgot, and (as teens often do) they began to think that they knew more than their mother. Humanity acted out, separating and failing to see their impact. But, Mother felt it. She was deeply impacted by this disconnection. Harmony and balance were lost. Faced with an empty nest, Mother Earth began to draw in and reassess her life and creations. Deep inner rebalancing and healing were needed.

Individualized and living separated, the young adults began feeling the changes and seeing new choices. Mother Earth, moving into the next phase of her own development, offered Humanity a new level of participation.

White Buffalo Calf woman, a Native American, brought the Sacred Pipe to North America as a gift to assist with Humanity's participation. Young Humanity smoked the sacred pipe, but did not remember. They did not remember the choice was to be breathed as a sacred pipe, to open up to the harmony and balance flowing through all creation, and reconnect to the web of all that is.

This story comes as a seed that is deep within the memory of Humanity. We are remembering, now, to actively participate. We are not separate. We are not connecting to the Sacred Pipe... we are the Sacred Pipe! Consciously coming together in all of the parts within each of us is the Earth/"Bowl"/Body and the Hollow Bone/Spirit, and all that flows through us.

In our separation we forgot who we were. "They" are "us." We are Earth; we are Nature; we are star beings and everything flowing through. There is no separation.

We stand at a precipice of choice. Our Mother Earth and Nature teach balance and harmony. Do we feel our impact? And reconnect to participate in a more balanced harmonious way? Do we open up our wholeness and bring ourselves into the bigger wholeness—as does a tree in the forest or a drop of water in the ocean? Will we move into a new balance of participation?

The next step in our evolutionary process...is to let go... of separation.

I lead to an ancient alliance, I orient, choose,
balance human and plant forces…

*Oberto Airaudi, "Falco"

There are no skies brighter
than those lit by the awareness of plants,
alive with changes, discoveries and hopes,
oriented by magical human knowledge…

*Oberto Airaudi, "Falco"

See

by Mariénne Kreitlow

the way trees hug the hills
spreading out generous roots into places we can't see.
they hold the hillside firmly.
stately trunks reach into branches,
modeling how to stand with dignity.
let us walk in morning light over frosty grass,
down gravel roads girded by aromatic ditches;
while others glide over cool mosque floors;
stride down long halls of schools;
duck under jungle's overhanging mazes;
strike heels on city sidewalks in polyphonic clacking.
mustang may pound up dust in hidden canyons
and mountain goats jig high into perilous skies
—but it's roots, deep roots, hold us all.

move with me over our kitchen floor
now, before I sweep, grit sticking to our feet,
or outside into gardens where autumn swallows summer,
to the coop to scatter feed to chattery, pecking chickens.
let us stand and watch the old garage collapse molecule
        by molecule
into a cracked yet obstinate foundation for another twenty years
        or more
—just as last year's pup, now huge in mass and joy, nearly bowls
        us over.

intertwine your roots with mine
inside this budding morn
standing as a grove with trees that hug the hills.

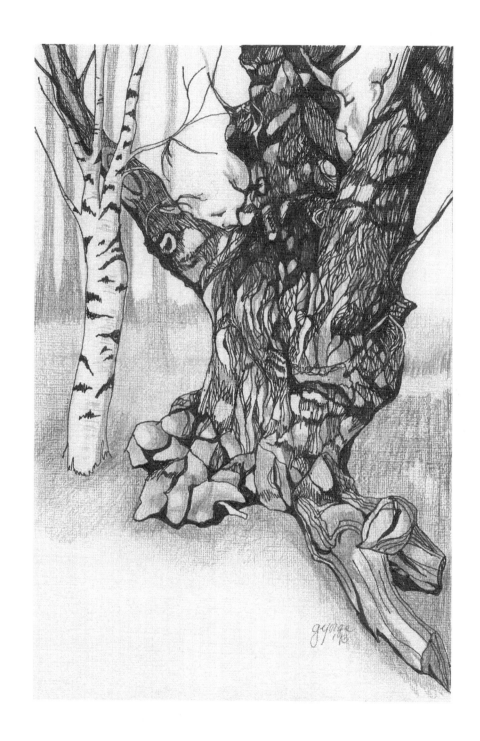

Roots Remain

by Lauren Robins
illustrated by Gyorge Ann Wecker Yawn

He was like oak. Strong, focused, and anchored for family, friends, and community. With a 'hard bark' presence—perhaps the result of the limiting soil of the awful war years and poverty, both financial and emotional—he created tight rings of stoicism.

I, his daughter, was like birch, playful and light and excited by life's delicious palette. As we both grew deeper into our rootedness, our energies clashed. Whereas my life tilted into the breeze, his anchored into the taproot of tradition. There were times when I tried to loosen the tight rings he kept around his heart by my dancing playfulness, but his unyielding nature stood fast. Generations create difference.

Now, I'm remembering myself at seven years old; it was just the two of us taking a car ride to a town nearby to visit his sister. It is fall in the Northeast and the trees are shimmering their colorful hues of autumnal animation. In rapt amazement, I am listening to my father's deep and soft voice offering "Trees" by Joyce Kilmer.

> I think that I shall never see
> A poem as lovely as a tree.
> A tree whose hungry mouth is pressed
> Against the Earth's sweet flowing breast;
> A tree that looks at God all day,
> And lifts her leafy arms to pray;
> A tree that in summer wears
> A nest of robins in her hair;
> Upon whose bosom snow has lain;
> Who intimately lives with rain.
> Poems are made by fools like me,
> But only God can make a tree.

Still, after sixty-plus years, I hold that memory close through all our years of differing dimensions. It is through "Trees" that I was able to know of his softness, his vulnerability, his "birchness." Poetry offers that. Since he did teach me about focus and about being an anchor for many, I honor his support, and I realize the acorn does not fall far. I believe I offer that. I lift my arms to pray that oak and birch have interlaced, creating roots for a tree that will yield fruition for generations to come.

Waking Tree

by Ann Marie Molnar

The first bird calls me.
Her sharp, clear note slices through the stillness
of a March morning
severing winter from spring.
She is the first of all the birds to summon the sap
from my roots.

My wakeup call.

My long body tingles with rising fluids,

stretching little by little.
If not for her song
I would take my slow and syrupy time
arousing from sleep.
If not for her song,
my sap would rest longer beneath the ground.
But she has come to remind me.

It's time.

Her music draws my fluids

to the very tips of my twigs
like fingers reaching out
unraveling in sunshine, wind, and water-drops.
My buds burgeon with dreams
of the leaves to come.
Like dendrites my branches reach
longing for wild synapses of light,

small green flames of excitement,
the dance of happy chlorophyll.

It's her song that draws the music out of me.

There will be more like her to come,

singing songs of different kinds,
their harmonies blending.
They are my symphonies.

You think that birds sing only for each other,
think again.
They sing for us.
How else would our leaves stretch forth,
our blossoms unfurl,
our pollen spin its golden DNA and burst forth?

Think again.

The birds themselves dance
in my branches
I feel my body move as they move.
I feel every note of their songs,
every nuance of breeze that strokes my leaves.

If you think that I do not feel,
think again.

Every cell in my body rises to spring,
every cell luxuriates in the density of summer.
Every cricket and katydid thrums
in my own vegetal neurons.

As Below,
my roots drive through dark loam,
around rocks and stones, seeking nutrients.

As Above,
my twigs send tree thoughts into the heavens.
At night, when you are sleeping,
we breathe our dreams into your hearts.

If you think we do not dream,
think again.
Our dreams bring moisture to the sky,
air into the world.
You will hear the birds and the crickets
but you do not hear our songs outright.
Our music sails forth on petal wind
and bird wing.
Our music sinks into your skin
whether you know it or not.
If you think you do not feel us,
think again.

Grandfather Tree

written and illustrated by Joni James

My little four-year-old body was shaking with fear. Not only was it a dark, moonless night, but the blustery, winter storm was making eerie howling noises through the house. There was another sound, too. The screaming sounded like an old man in pain, calling out. In the room I shared with my sleeping little sister, I knelt on my pink flowered pillow and peered through the Venetian blinds into the darkness outside. I was looking for the howling wolf, who was figuring out a way to climb up into my second-floor bedroom to eat me. I still don't know how I found the courage to look. I did not find the wolf, but I did see the maple tree outside my window thrashing it's limbs fiercely.

In the morning, I made a snowman with the new fallen snow. I climbed the lower branches of the leafless tree to get the last leaves that refused to fall the month before. Now crunchy and brown, they made great "hair" for my snow sculpture. I stood for a moment and wondered if the tree was hurt from the night before. It wasn't. I just knew.

The spring brought a lush, thick canopy of leaves that made shade for me to play in. The seeds were my favorite part. There were two seeds attached to a stem, and two odd leafy things, that make them fall in a twirling motion. Hence, the nickname "helicopters." We kids would also stick the helicopters in our mouths and use them as whistles. It never did really work very well, but it was many years before we gave up. We didn't have to give up, because the tree gave us many whistles and many helicopters and lots of shade to keep our tender skin cool and protected from the summer sun. It gave us branches to climb and a thick trunk to lean against—and there was even one branch that was bent so we could "ride" it like a horse.

That summer I laid in the thick, soft grass under the tree, finding animals in the clouds. It was almost my fifth birthday, and I was excited to be old enough to go to kindergarten. I was reciting the alphabet with difficulty, when I heard a sound similar to music. It was a rhythm that helped me remember which letter came next. I don't know how, but I knew it was the tree that I loved and feared so much "singing" to me.

My awareness of the maple tree became constant and easy. There was nothing magical about it. I loved it, and it loved me. I thought the tree was an old man, or that an old man lived within it, and I called him "Grandfather Tree." Many nights I would kneel on my bed and listen to his songs. During the day, they were soft whispers. I could hear him talking, but never knew his language. I only knew the sounds were mostly sweet and comforting unless there was a big storm. He did not like storms; he would groan and scream like an old man who was hurt. He was my friend. He was my tree, and I was his girl.

Decades after I moved from my childhood home, I returned to see that Grandfather Tree had grown so large that his roots had torn up the cement driveway and the lawn. That must be why the new owners cut Grandfather Tree down. Thankfully, souls never die. Not even in trees!

When I became a mother, it was because of my relationship with Grandfather Tree, and ensuing awareness of life forms all around us, that I decided to take my daughter's Girl Scout Troop 583 through the woods on a "treasure hunt." Their mission was to quietly look and listen. For some of these citified girls, this was their first romp through the woods. At nine, they were far more interested in exploring their transitioning world between Barbies and Malls, than being quiet.

"There's nothing here," whined one of the little green-capped darlings.

"Nothing?" I asked. I led them to the bank of a river. I had them line up with their arms spread, so there was plenty of no-talking room between them. "What do you see?" NOTHING said the exasperated child, wondering when we would get back to our cabin. I gave them an assignment: be quiet and watch. They finally all settled down into silence. Some found rocks to sit on. Some just stood at the edge of the river wondering what was so important that we had to remain so still. One asked if they were being punished!

After just three or four minutes of silence, the river sprang to life! Dragonflies flew over the surface, turtles popped their heads out of the water, tiny frogs, no bigger than a thumbnail, were clicking happily away. The scouts were straining to keep their voices hushed as, one by one, they heard and they saw! Bugs, snakes, fish, tadpoles, mosquitoes, flying things, crawly things and swimming things.

The little whiney one stood defiantly with her arms crossed, looking up. When she heard the others growing excited about their finds, she too had a moment of awe. Across the river was a hill packed with trees. Maple trees dressed in late spring green were waving in the wind. It looked like the ocean, in big waves, dancing in unison to the wind. "Look, they are dancing!" she exclaimed as she began swaying with the trees.

The other girls joined in, and soon they collapsed in a pile of giggles as they bumped into each other, and became trees looking more like they were in a hurricane than a late spring breeze!

As we gathered around the bonfire that night, with the requisite S'mores and marshmallow infernos, we talked about what they saw. One by one, they bragged about their little critter as if it were a chunk of gold they had found! We ended the night in the "Tree Dance" with all the girls from Troop 583 swaying like little drunken sailors on a moonlit night, laughing and swaying and bumping into one another.

Simple pleasures for simple times!

Of Japanese origin, haiku is poetry reduced to its simplest form. Haiku is believed to be the shortest form of poem we find in world literature. These haiku by Calen Rayne, throughout the book, were written spontaneously in the presence of trees around the world.

Winter woods,
barren branches,
a full moon rises…

      Calen Rayne

Cool river moonlight,
bright lightning paints a great oak.
Whispers of light rain.

      Calen Rayne

LOST

by Lillie Rowden

Small acorn fallen on dank, dark ground -
Viewed as an oak, uplifted on high,
Minute promise, a life to fulfill,
Towering against storm riven sky,
Branches torn in the wild wind's advance,
Twisted and tormented out of place,
Yet deep within the leaf shriven dance,
A strength, a beauty, visible grace.

Small acorn fallen on dank, dark ground -
Listening to rain's now gentle fall,
Awaiting secret promises within,
Covered in earth's light funeral pall,
Warmed and nurtured by the risen sun,
Caught, treasured in creation's embrace,
The battle for life is swift begun -
The green new promise reveals its face.

Small acorn fallen on dank, dark ground -
Spark of new joy with courage to dare!
Reminding my soul, God's love profound
Redeemed the lost with infinite care,
Lifted, fulfilling its destiny,
Towering shade from dark forest space,
Guarding small creatures, entrusted high,
Its branches directed, shaped by God's grace.

Breathed by Tree

by Shiila Clear Tree
illustrated by Faith Harrison

P ain shot up my back as I slowly walked to my Vision Quest
site, while escorted by two loving supporters. My sacred
walking stick helped bear my weight with each step, min-
imizing the pain. It was decorated with brightly colored cloth
and feathers, and would double as the door, or entrance to my
Vision Quest circle. These same supporters had supported me in
my year-long preparation for my Vision Quest, and would check
on my safety while I was out. I was silently praying that a few days
of lying directly on the Earth would heal my back. A magnificent
90-foot loblolly pine was guardian over my site. He called me to
spend this time of fasting, praying, and silence with him. I felt
honored, and filled with anticipation.

Once alone in my circle of prayer ties†, I stood with the elderly pine I called "Grandfather." I leaned my back against his
bark, rocking gently on either side of my spine. I felt so cared for,
rocked by the Tree Spirit. I stood this way long enough to feel
a connection with him. Then I got the message to connect my
heart and back through the breath. I breathed into my heart and
on the exhale sent the breath and the energy down my spine to

---

† In the Earthtribe spiritual community, we tie prayer ties as part of our
preparation for a Vision Quest. We have adopted the Lakota tradition of tying
405 ties, honoring the Nature Spirits in their landscape. We place tobacco,
sage and other natural items in a small square of cotton cloth, say a prayer
over each one, and string them all together with cotton string. When we arrive
at our Vision Quest site, we roll out the prayer ties to create a circle that defines
the physical boundaries for our time of fasting and praying. We sit inside this
circle of protection for the length of our stay. The Vision Quest is a time of
solitude in nature, free of the demands of our busy lives. The Vision Quester
seeks a vision on behalf of the tribe as well as for her own personal growth.

my lower back. I did that while praying for Grandfather to help me be straight and tall like he was. I followed his lead, imagining that I too had roots extending beyond my physical body down into the Earth. I reached down, sending my energy through my roots into the Earth through the base of my spine and bottom of my feet. Then I opened myself to receiving nourishment through my roots, using my breath as a tool. On an inhale, I breathed in nurturing Earth energy and brought it up to my heart. Following Grandfather Pine, I reached up to the sky, and felt this healing energy flow up through me.

An awareness came upon me to open my heart to receive energy from Grandfather, and send that down my spine to my lower back and tailbone. I breathed like that for a while, gently rocking. I knew that a healing was taking place. When it was time to stop, I turned around and put my forehead against his bark, thanking him. Then I heard words floating in my mind, "You are a teacher. It is your way to share what you learn, to teach others through your experiences. This is for more than you alone. Share my wisdom with the community. Many experiences will be given to you in order for you to learn valuable lessons for the greater whole. Lie down at my feet and we will continue our conversation."

I lay down on my back with my knees bent, with my head up against the tree so that the top of my head was against the bark and I was looking straight up the trunk. I settled into the soft pine needle bed and asked Grandmother Earth to flow her energy through my body to bring balance and healing. I breathed like that for a while, as I delightfully watched three hawks and one "Peace Eagle" (also known as a turkey vulture) fly overhead. I felt like the tree was growing out of the top of my head.

Then I had the knowing that Earth energy and the Feminine were in my body as it curved with bent knees. I became the Sacred Pipe†, with my body as the bowl of the pipe, the top of my

† "The Sacred Pipe" is a respectful term for the Native American pipe, which is a spiritual artifact, or holy object used for individual prayer or community

head the place where bowl and stem meet, and Grandfather Pine the stem of the pipe, straight and tall. I felt the joining of Masculine and Feminine energies at the top of my head. I felt my belly open to receive, like the bowl receives the sacred tobacco. I felt my body as Earth, and felt an energy flow from Earth to Sky through me, then through Grandfather Tree. I knew then how important it is to send good energy, clear thinking, and positive aspirations up the stem to be carried to Great Spirit.

A raven flew and circled directly over Grandfather and me. A tufted titmouse landed on the branch nearby. Then its mate arrived. One flew to the bark of the tree just above my head and talked to me. He did that twice, and then once again later. A message I got from the titmouse was "When you are still, everything comes to you." When he repeated this again later, I wondered if his nest was close by and he was actually asking me to leave.

While I was lying down being the Sacred Pipe, I felt and heard a pop in my lower back, and knew that it had gone back into place. I was very grateful for my Earth Mother chiropractic adjustment! I looked up at a rustle in the woods, and saw a coyote walking through an opening on the other side of the creek, accompanied by the squawks of ravens. I felt invisible. I was embodied Earth. I stayed this way until the chill of the night suggested I get up and prepare for full dark.

The next morning I was greeted by Owl, my guardian and protector with whom I spent the dark night. I visited Grandfather Pine again, positioning myself at the foot of the great tree with my back on Mother Earth, the top of my head touching the bark of the tree, and my knees bent. I heard the message, "Focus on the

---

ritual. It is at the heart of Native American spirituality, as it helps the people connect with the divine. The smoke from the pipe carries the prayers to the Creator, Great Spirit, or Sacred Mystery, and provides the path for Great Spirit to travel to Earth.

breath through the heart. Breathe into the heart, then let go of control of your breath and let me "breathe you."

It is difficult to describe in words the feeling of 'being breathed by the tree.' It was very subtle. An energy channel had opened, and there was an exchange taking place between us. I lost track of where I ended and he began, as these words floated through my mind, "Remember the connection is through the breath and physical touch. Right now the opening in the top of your head touching my bark is the channel for me to 'breathe you.' Before, it was as you leaned on my trunk. I have ancient wisdom to pass on to you and other humans that can listen and receive. Opening the communication between Tree People and humans is essential for the survival of the human race. We have suffered great losses, because our family has been destroyed. We are aware of a great loss in Bastrop†. We breathe for you. We breathe out oxygen which humans need to survive. The number of trees is greatly reduced, and the number of people on Earth is steadily increasing. The ratio is changing. It is very important to pay attention to the tree-to-human ratio. When there are mass deaths due to fire, earthquake, volcano, tsunami, floods, and tornadoes, Earth is balancing out this ratio again. As I said yesterday, you are given this information to share with your community. Community is essential for humans to survive, because of the Earth changes that are coming. Community is natural law. Our tree community is strongly connected across the Earth—even if we are greatly diminished.

"The Earth has gone through similar changes before, and life was lost. Now, the involvement of humans complicates things.

---

† Bastrop State Park conserved a large pine forest, about 35 miles east of Austin, Texas, which tragically suffered from a fire that raged for five weeks and burned 33,000 acres in 2011. The fire destroyed the old growth trees which were the westernmost stand of loblolly pines in the United States. To restore the "Lost Pines," Texas Parks and Wildlife Department and Texas State Forest Service are planting more than four million trees on public and private lands.

The relationship between humans and the rest of life needs to change if humans are to survive. We living beings are constantly communicating and collaborating with one another. This includes rocks, Earth, wind, sun, stars, moon, winged ones, and four-leggeds. We are all here on Earth together. Welcome to the conversation. There is good work being done in Europe and now here too. Native Peoples knew about this balance, and now the balance needs to be restored once again.

"The Tree People welcome communication with humans. We have much knowledge to share with you. This is enough for now. Come back and we will do this again."

My heart was full of gratitude. I noticed that my chest felt open and spacious, like there was more room inside than ever before. I marveled at the healing that occurred in my back. I felt humbled before this great tree, and honored to be chosen to receive such an important message, as I am honored to pass it on to you now. Over the next few days, Grandfather Pine continued to give me good counsel, which I have taken to heart in my life. I have found a wise, old teacher. I know that my experience of being breathed by this guardian tree has altered me in a profound way. It was as if the message was transmitted through the breath, directly into the cells of my body. It holds the promise and the key to a more intimate relationship with all trees. For this I am grateful.

The nature name given to me after this Vision Quest was "Clear Tree." This is my name to live into for the next leg of my journey. I feel both challenged and honored by this task, as its meaning continues to unfold and make itself known in my life.

I orient human, powerful minds,
to their natural
forgotten task:
the harmony of all, the living whole
that requires the consent of the green species...
— Oberto Airaudi, "Falco"

I lead thoughts and emotions, dreams,
to the mission that the human species must realize,
a new covenant, a celestial ritual
toward the living plants of our shared world...

— Oberto Airaudi, "Falco"

Breathed by Tree part two

by Shiila Clear Tree

Exploring the breathing practice with the tree
First breathing into my heart and out of my heart
Third-eye touching the tree
Hands hugging the tree in contact with the bark/skin
Then releasing my breath to the tree, asking "Will you breathe
    me? I surrender my breath to you."
Very subtle awareness of breathing from third-eye contact point,
    then hands and legs and sense of all over air exchange not
    focused on one part of the body
Glimpse of non-local sense
Skin breathing, bark breathing connection
Shift in awareness
Bigger perspective
Being breathed by Spirit
Sense of being part of a greater whole
My physical body an extension of a living breathing energy
    of life; non-local
Everywhere at once alive
A shift from my one-pointed focus, my sense of origination
From small mind to BIG mind
Again a sense of letting go of boundaries, of separation
To open out to something so much larger moving through me
Sensed physically and energetically with the assistance of the tree
    as my guide
Now breathing with me like a pulsing breath of life
Breathing us both
I feel a sense of peace, like being held in loving arms
Breathing together
Free of time and space
Breathed by Spirit

A Tribute to a Mighty Oak

by Steve Lingle

illustrated by Cheryl Elms

This story started long ago. The cycle of life caused an acorn to form which, in turn, grew into a tree. This tree started like every other tree of its type: from acorn to tiny sprig with one or two leaves, then gradually growing over the years into a sapling, and finally maturing into a fully developed red oak towering over the surrounding landscape. I have become a devotee of this tree as I gradually became aware of its immense presence. I live in a woods, and this tree is in my back yard.

I have always loved trees. When I was young I would climb to the highest branch of the biggest tree and look out over the world from high above the ground. Later on, when I was in college, I studied forestry and dendrology and learned about trees and how to identify the different types. It amazes me to think that a tiny twig can sprout from an acorn, or a hickory nut, or a walnut and grow into this enormous, living, breathing entity that we call a tree.

Several hundred years ago this region of the Earth was originally made up of hardwood forest. Most of the land was cleared, long before I was born, to make farmland. Fortunately, there are areas that have been protected, not too far away, where I can walk in a forest of what is called "old growth." It always makes me feel good to walk in a forest. I can become lost in the feeling, especially in the spring, when the forest is coming alive with new growth. When I walk in one of these old growth forests I can feel the energy and life force of the Earth. I get a sense of timelessness, and ages that have passed. Nature is impervious to the comings and goings of man. I know that if left alone, if unchecked by the hand of man, this whole region of Earth would revert into hardwood forest.

I live in a small patch of woods in farm country, surrounded by fields that are full of beans and corn during the growing season. I have lived here for a long time in human years—almost 25 years—enough time to learn to resonate with the natural environment that surrounds my home. It is a rural area, but there are neighbors not too far away, and at night you can see the lights of the towns and cities that are nearby.

On this small patch of Earth that I call home I have my very own forest; it is my "nature experiment." I call it my "experiment" because when my wife and I moved here there were no small trees. The previous owner had cows and they ate all the small trees. So when we moved in, there were only big trees. We have let nature reclaim this little patch of woods naturally without interference for 25 years, the only exception being a trail that leads to the back part of the woods where we have our garden. I have watched groves of saplings grow to form a canopy that has risen up under the shelter of the old trees. These young trees have grown until they now shade the Earth, and keep the woods cool on a hot summer day.

Roughly in the middle of our woods stands a huge oak tree, and for many years I didn't grasp the size of this tree. Then one day I realized that it's upper branches would hit the roof of my house if it fell, and I started taking a really good look at how truly big it was. This tree is enormous; it's branches spread and lift high, filling the sky. Many years ago, all of its smaller branches broke and fell off during a serious ice storm, so that now the main branches are all that remain. Recently, an arborist came to see the tree and assured me that it was over two hundred years old. It is a tree that I call "The Mighty Oak."

The first time I felt the presence of this tree was on a warm summer night some years ago. I was out walking in the dark of the night sky. It was warm enough to stroll without a jacket. I was walking on the trail that leads to the back of the woods and the garden. It was a beautiful night for a walk and I was enjoying the gentle breeze. There was an occasional rustle of leaves, and the hum of insects could be heard talking in the night. Gradually my senses synchronized in tune with the energy emanating from the forest.

There is an opening in the woods that we use for wiener roasts. It was there that I felt a flowing energy as I gazed upward and beheld the immense oak. Overcome by the feeling, I raised my arms and let this energy flow through me and up through the tree. From that spot, the night sky fills with the silhouette of this mighty oak, and it was there that I "talked" with the tree for the first time, and gave thanks to Mother Earth.

"Oh Mighty Oak, you stand in silent splendor, majestic and tall, your branches fill the sky. What changes have occurred during your watch? You were alive when the forests were cleared for timber, and the land was scraped clean to make farmland for planting crops. You watched roads being built and houses pop up all around you...and still you stand. What a story you might tell if you could talk.

"I am awed by your silent splendor. As I gaze up and up and further up to the top of your branches, I marvel at your immense size. I can feel the energy of the Earth reaching out and coursing through you. As I stand before you, I am filled with gratitude and respect. As I reach my arms up to you I give thanks for a God that would create such a magnificent living being. When I stand before you, Mighty Oak, and look up at your soaring heights, I can feel the energy of life and I am filled with Love and I know peace.

"Looking up into your vast heights I know that there is a great power at work. I can sense the life force that is the creator of all things. I know that the same life force that courses through your branches is the same life force that courses through my veins, and is the same life force that is the creator of all things, of Gaia, of the universe, of the cosmos.

"I am grateful to share this small plot of Earth with you. I give thanks to the essence of life that would create such a magnificent Earth, such breathtaking sunrises and sunsets, such beauty as the changing of the seasons, and something as wondrous as you, oh huge red oak tree."

And so I find myself in the unpleasant position of having to choose between a tree and a house. The arborist who visited, after much measuring, determined that the upper 30 feet of branches will indeed hit my house when the tree falls. Over the last few years several large trees have fallen. It seems like the storms are getting stronger here, with higher gusts of wind; or perhaps the older trees have reached the age when it is time for them to make way for the younger trees. Whatever the reason, the huge red oak which was once the biggest of all the trees in the forest, now stands mostly alone. Most of the big trees surrounding it have blown down. I know it is only a matter of time before the Mighty Oak also succumbs to the forces of high winds and gravity.

Since moving here, my philosophy has been to let mother nature reclaim this small patch of ground as she sees fit. I have planted many trees which thrive, one of each local variety, so cutting down a tree that is still alive goes against my principles. I have considered stringing cables from the Mighty Oak to other large trees, but it wouldn't be practical. It would cause too much interference. It is just the Mighty Oak's time.

It is sad for me to have to make this decision. I would rather let nature decide when and how this tree releases its life energy, but because of its proximity to my house—I can't. In some way, it is fitting that my first conversation with the forest was with this tree. For many years, before I was able to perceive the life force emanating from it, it was just a big tree. There are many other trees that I have resonated with since then, but this oak was the first. This story is my way of giving thanks to the Mighty Oak. It is my tribute and my way of asking for forgiveness, for interfering. I know this is something that must be done. It is part of the turning of the wheel of life. Thanks for listening.

She Tree

by Larry Winters

It was the wind that called me to her.

It may have carried her scent,

or caused her to tremble slightly for me to see,

or delivered her inviting whisper.

I went to her

lay my head in her lap.

she shared beauty, and wisdom.

I lay my hand on her body,

she urged gentleness.

I lightened my touch,

felt my soul lifted.

Soft words I'd never dared speak, spiraled out.

No barriers, no resistance, no confusions,

love, true, all one hundred feet.

The Loving Nature of Anticipation

written and illustrated by Sharon Carter

Memory fails to include a significant portion of my fading history, yet remarkable stories are rationed from the margins which I do glean and relish. This is a tender recollection which offered me a bit of peace, even vulnerability and healing.

It's about a tree.

I grew up in a new subdivision that inserted itself like a long finger into a deep wood. The tall trees were oak and dogwood and maple and birch and tulip, and in the fall they shed their leaves in a shower of color upon our lawn. Just a handful of elfin pines were scattered throughout the understory, gripping their evergreen foliage as seasons changed.

I was a child of the woods. I loved the woods. I loved the trees and the sticks and the stones and the creek. I had a special rock I would sit upon while I imagined being the protagonist in stories thin in plot, but woodsy in depth.

One wintry December, while sitting on my rock, I thought about the approaching Christmas. Santa Claus brought our Christmas tree together with our presents on Christmas Eve—after we went to bed. My friends already had trees in their houses. I was a child that loved anticipation even more than Christmas Day.

And I needed a tree to anticipate.

This probably stands out in memory because for the first time in my young life, I did something other than what my mother traditionally controlled and directed. I twisted and broke off a small scraggly pine branch near my rock, and set it up in our house like my own tiny tree.

I then sat down at my little art table and spent every spare moment drawing Christmas ornaments—even the hooks—which I cut out and hung on the tiny tree. I invited the whole family to enjoy my tree—and dedicated it as their tree, too!

My mother was gracious, and let me put the tree on the floor by the big chair in the living room. It was barely taller than the arm of the chair. When presents arrived in the mail from relatives, they were placed around my tree.

Each day I made more ornaments.

I sat on the floor by my tree as I did homework, played games, made gifts, sang carols of baby Jesus, and dreamed of Christmas. I poured my love and attention onto that little branch which bore my anticipation and delight. I was very satisfied.

Mother even allowed my brother, sister and I to open the packaged gifts around the tiny tree on some evenings, and our ensuing laughter enhanced its purpose all the more!

This was a wonderful tree.

Then Christmas Day arrived along with Santa's tree sparkling with tinsel and glory, and surrounded by an immense wealth of presents. It was placed in a different room. The excitement of the day excluded the now dried and withered branch.

Anticipation was over.

But the child in me is a sentimental sort of soul, with a soft heart for any of God's living creations. I asked my parents if I could plant my tiny tree in the backyard.

My folks played along. They considered the branch a stick, which after a few weeks in the house, seemed quite dead. It was planted in the cold hard clay ground of winter.

Even so, this story became my mother's extraordinary story years later...

...Whenever she showed anyone the lofty pine tree that grew in our backyard!

Reflecting back on my years as a young girl, I recall that I held dear a wide assortment of things, alive or inanimate. My perspective was not the big picture, but the details, each with intimate importance and filled with my appreciation.

Like the ornaments bestowed on my tiny tree, I would make art to show I cared. The creative task of art is problematic to accomplish...a committed journey from heart to finish. During the process of making art, I spent considerable time and attention devoted to projecting genuine goodwill toward the recipient. Artwork was my emotional and spiritual demonstration of love.

The result was given away.

To this day, I doubt family members grasp the honest heart of my handmade presents, but the intention remains as pure as anything can attain to be in this broken world...the intention. Poor at small talk, introvert to the core, this was my communication that at least offered an uncorrupted relationship.

With the same reasoning, whatever came into my life back then was considered a valuable gift from God, mother, grandma, aunty, or friend...I felt honored by the butterfly emerging from his cocoon on my rock, or the nail file I unwrapped from grandma. Time was slow and I grew up in one place feeling safe...and relatively bored...which granted me space for attachments.

Motivation is primal in humans. It was not an unselfish act to pluck the branch because I wanted a tree. However, I treated my "broken" branch as a tiny tree, and believed that it was open to receiving "heart-fed" nourishment. What happened that empowered the branch to overcome death is a mystery. Yet this mystery provided all that was needed to grow a "whole" tree!

There is a wise adage, which states that we understand things "the way we are," not the way things really are. Focusing on what we choose to see, the balance is ignored or despised or feared... "cognitive dissonance." I truly cannot comprehend the immense nature of what holds us together in this universe, because I realize that I know so little.

And growing older, my outlook was destined for distortion by the world.

After I left home for college, I kept leaving my new homes, on the move, beckoning constant changes, shedding security.

My adult years were focused on attaining and surviving the drama of relationships, challenges of the day, and events of life. I am sad to say that the meaningful account of a cherished branch that became a tree, did not move with me in depth or spirit.

It was ignored.

Anticipation turned to anxiety when my role changed from waiting for Santa to playing Santa. The initiation of the season began with the Christmas tree my children craved, and that tree symbolically bore my stress, so that I could carry on with the burden of performing holiday expectations.

I have not had a favorite tree since my Christmas "branch."

During the years when I lived on Maui, I nurtured a potted Cooks Pine for which I began a holiday tradition of making an assortment of ornaments, after scavenging the tropical flora of the island. The first year, I picked bean pods from the Willi Willi trees on the deserted south road to Kaupo. The beans were a bright blaze orange. I shelled them, glued and hooked them, and dipped them in lacquer.

One or two continue to find their way onto my Christmas trees, now loaded with family memorabilia thirty-some years later. Because no one helps me decorate, I feel alone with this "chore." My grown kids make fun of the Willi Willi beans.

It was while reading a short story by a nineteenth-century French writer, Guy de Maupassant, that I came across an astonishing perspective on trees. In his tale, a group of old world villagers were sitting by a cottage fireplace one evening, sharing grog, puffing on pipes, and discussing their fear of the forest around them. It was their conviction that the world was not made for people—because there were so many trees!

This posture grabbed my attention.

My first notion was that those clueless villagers had no idea that the trees sucked up the poisonous carbon dioxide they exhaled, and in turn, provided the pure fresh oxygen which sustained their very lives…they needed trees to live! They were in a crucial relationship, which they had no idea existed.

I then confronted myself on whether I could admit fearing or despising or even ignoring something which could be, in fact, saving my life. Some mystery?

Surely, as I live and breathe, the answer is "yes." I had even forgotten the loving anticipation I had with a broken branch, which became a tree. I left that story behind. But now, in this season of my life, it has reached forward to offer a touchstone to serenity in an anxious world.

I confess that, as a human being, I cannot really accomplish anything "alone"—for that reason, we are all saved by love. Support lifts us higher. So I did not make the "aha" connection by myself. Friends germinated an idea for a book, extended an invitation, and triggered a thought. I searched through the vast realm designated to my history, and into corners of memory—which I had, indeed, ignored for some time. Opening up my mind to see beyond my current conflicting circumstances, I dusted off a buried treasure…

As I began to write about the broken branch—my tiny Christmas tree—a child was set free from captivity to tell me what she saw, how she saw it, and what happened.

Sharing her story became a sweet gift to myself: Our lives absolutely depend on how we treat ourselves, each other, and the world around us. It is a crucial relationship.

And I see that God's intention is beauty and life. Waiting to become perfectly whole. Surely that is why we were created to love that which is "broken"...

The Mystery is His intention.

Snow covered trees,
the sound of an oar
striking still waters.

       Calen Rayne

Alone in fresh snow
I wander aimlessly through
empty, twisted branches...

       Calen Rayne

the olive tree

by Quaglia

my tree is an olive tree
from the air, breathing in the infinity of sky, free clear and light
roots twist and entwine in the fertile depths of the earth
leaves purify thoughts and whisper the rhythm of time
moving in a contained dance with the wind

ancient rich tree
reflecting the nature of your land
microcosm of solid vitality

Tuscany
most saturated of all the earthly paradises I have seen
fire of life distilled from the sun in rays of light
pure gold

golden, the sunflowers
golden, the fruit trees
the cherry, fig, apricot and plum

every object you contain
everything created and touched in you
a natural expression of beauty
Renaissance potency in every courtyard and chapel
vital and creative incision

your people, armed with smiles of innocence and joy
pleasure in the air, in La Maremma
from the sea, up to the hills, into the vineyards
I could spend a lifetime going around your roads
lined with cypress and oak

In Regello
surrounded by bright, red poppy flowers
interrupting the infinite green with kisses of passionate color
in the fields with beans and potatoes,
strawberries and cabbage
I feel at home on this faraway land
agricultural outpost charged with light, thought and intention

spiritual brothers and sisters with luminous eyes
like the azure of the sea
every dinner a simple and delectable party
every drop of oil and wine, worthy of a queen

at sunset, leaning against the trunk of the olive tree
my tree, it envelops me with poetry
subtle nourishment, the wisdom of this sacred earth

 inspired by Damanhur nucleo community *Netila Ra* in Tuscany

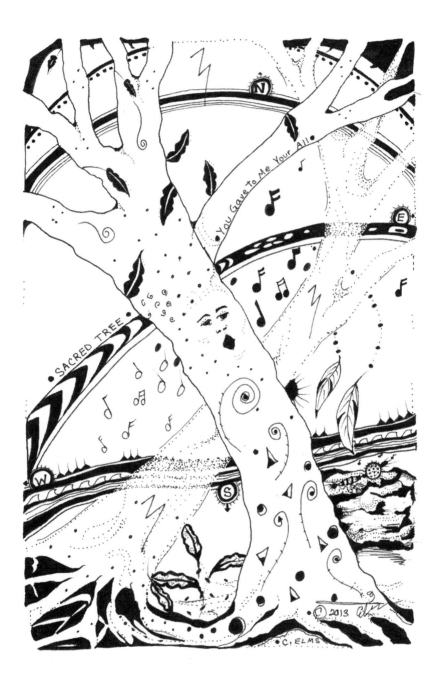

The Tree of Many Voices

by Deborah Doblado Bowers
illustrated by Cheryl Elms

*"Once we perceive there is sacred energy, spark or spirit
in everything around us, we realize that we inhabit a
sacred world."*

Jean Shinoda Bolen

Early in my relationship with the *Earthtribe*, a nature-based
spiritual community, a personal daily practice arose, one
taking me deep into my soul to meet the voices and shadows within. I began by sitting at the base of a Shumard oak tree
in my backyard. This red oak of three trunks and far reaching
branches provided abundant shade. The porch steps led down to
a path right to the tree where I created a medicine wheel to honor the eight directions practiced by the tribe: East, South, West,
North, Earth, Sky, Relations and Ancestors. A safe container was
created: a space and place to voice what was on my mind, free
from judgment.

It felt awkward, at first, to sit and talk to a tree. Soon, I began to feel its strength as I sensed the tree listening quietly to all
I had to say. I found stability, and felt rooted and grounded, as
I was invited to go deeper. In the quiet morning hours I started
to notice my surroundings, to see things I had not seen, to touch
what I had not touched. The view sitting at the base of the tree was
different from where I normally perched, high upon the porch.
The sounds were sweeter, the sights more distinct.

The birds sang the morning into being. Cricket frogs hopped
about, encouraging cleansing. A dung beetle carried a heavy load
up the side of a railroad tie, determined to get the job done. I saw

the yellowish underbelly of a woodpecker and experienced the stillness of a hummingbird. A broad winged hawk answered my call. White-tailed deer watched in wonder with large round eyes. I considered the unwavering mission of a possum and learned the importance of staying focused, staying on track.

The tree was patient, listening quietly, waiting for me to trust enough to reach deeper. The wildlife continued their supportive messages. One day I found a frightened little girl within, one I knew well in childhood, when we lived with an alcoholic parent. At first all she did was cry, so I held her in my arms, creating a safe container for her. Remembering the lessons of the tree and the relations, I patiently sat in silence waiting. When she felt comfortable and safe, she opened up and I listened. All she wanted was to be seen, to be heard, and to be loved. As her fears disappeared, we merged into one, making room for more voices to be heard.

Another day the critic appeared, then the judge. The perfectionist, among other strong personalities, came to visit. I listened and spoke with each, asking what they wanted, why they were here. Their angry voices were loud at first. I had ignored them for so many years. It took time to get to know each one, to listen, to accept, to face and embrace one another. We talked, cried and laughed together. I discovered many hidden selves, lost voices I had not heard clearly before. Some were fearful, some angry, some quiet, and some confused. One by one, I began to develop a relationship with these voices, to witness their pain, to know and accept them as part of who I am. The process put me on a path to becoming more whole, more complete, and more confident.

With practice and attention, I learned to listen with different ears, to hear the many voices within me. With guidance from my mentor, I learned to create a sacred council to work with my many selves. A deeply intimate relationship grew over time with what I call the "Tree of Many Voices."

Then one early September, there was a fierce storm, and our relationship changed. Following is an excerpt from my journal about this experience:

September 10, 2010: Tree of Many Voices, today is ceremony day. I grieve your loss a full three days now, not quite knowing what to do. I watch the deer feed on the leaves of your fallen branches. The squirrels appear numb, like me, wondering how this could be. Where is my companion, my confidant, my dear friend, the red oak tree of multiple trunks for climbing and far reaching branches for swinging? Where is the shade I sat beneath, the trunks I embraced, and the friend who introduced me to my many selves? Where have you gone?

John O'Donohue writes about "Anam Cara...a soul-friendship." This we share dear Tree of Many Voices, this and more. Your rootedness guides me in meditations as I sit at your base. There, I created a medicine wheel as I prepared for my first vision quest. There, you spoke to me in voices I did not know. There, I learned to ground myself to the Earth as you did with your roots. Your roots, your roots are now ripped from the Earth by a storm in the night! There lies a hole in their place, and a hole in my heart.

When did we begin this journey? It was nearly summer of 2007, wasn't it? Yes, I had just returned from Indiana and my son's wedding. It was Memorial Day weekend. That first day back, I was surprised by Nature with a lightning storm on my morning walk. I had just finished reading *Nature and Intimacy*, a book by J. Yost and W. Taegel on relationships. In it, I learned of meditating with trees and decided to try it.

What a journey this three years has been. You have been at my side throughout my identity search, through the fears, the voices, the lessons, the wisdom. I will miss you, dear one, my companion, and my guide. I will miss the sturdiness of your trunks, teaching me how to stand tall and strong, supported by Mother Earth and the rootedness of our connection. I will miss your branches reaching far and wide toward Father Sky, welcoming the opportunities that come. I will miss your fall leaves of red and orange, the many varieties of spring green, and the first tiny buds popping out, quickly filling the Sky with your beauty. I will miss the rustling sound of your leaves in the wind.

How many birds have I come to know sitting on your branches, singing the day into being; and squirrels with their bushy tails, chasing each other, flying from branch to branch. I am not the only one who will miss you, dear Oak. You are a friend to the many Relations who have come to teach me and to enjoy the spaciousness of your presence.

Upon arriving home, midday last Tuesday, I vividly recall looking out the wall of windows and being filled with wonder at the expansiveness of the Sky and the distant trees. The sensation is one of opening, opening, and opening—my theme to welcome the summer season. I blow the conch every day, honoring this feeling of openness, and here it is in my backyard, a big wide-open space. I am enthralled by the sensation. It takes me a few minutes to realize you are no longer standing there. Stepping out on the back porch, my heart sinks, seeing you lying there on your side. In the same moment, this expansive feeling is filling me up. It is hard to be sad with such a gift.

I decide to perform a ceremony this day to honor the Tree of Many Voices. Not sure where to begin, I walk through the house allowing the energy of the items that wish to participate to speak to me, including the clothes I am to wear. I gather all my feathers: owl, red-tailed hawk, turkey, red cardinal, and others found along my travels in Nature. I place them on the prayer rug that I lay upon the Earth, between the fallen trunks. I add a conch shell, a vision quest rattle, my journal and pen, a large healing drum, a little white stone buffalo, and a clear green container of water. Seeking direction through a few minutes of grounding meditation, I am led to pick up my rattle and rouse the energy of the moment; singing the tree and me awake, moving up and down the trunks, the branches, the roots, the leaves and all around the tree. I move slowly with focused attention as my feet find their way along the rocky and challenging path.

I circle four times in a moon-wise orbit, delivering healing potions with a compassionate feminine touch, through the sound of rattle and smoke of burning sage. Next, utilizing the water and the feathers, I move in a sun-wise circle to include the masculine energy of release and transformation. A new chant bubbles forth, "Ho Tree, Sacred Tree, I am here to honor you. Ho Tree, Sacred Tree, I am here in gratitude. Ho Tree Sacred Tree, you gave to me your all. Ho Tree, Sacred Tree, I will remember you."

I blow the conch four times, sitting on each of her trunks, and embracing her leaves. Then I settle upon the Earth, in my usual meditative place and pose, and loose myself in a drumming meditation.

I had placed the conch, rattle and feathers on a nearby rock. When I open my eyes, I see one of the feathers blowing away. Picking it up, I discover a set of owl feathers are missing, a precious gift from a supporter. Checking the assorted feathers twice, I do not find them. Crawling low on hands and knees, I search and search the ground, the branches, everywhere. The loss of these sacred feathers is almost too much too bear. The tears flow. Again and again, I search the whole of the tree, singing the feathers to return to me, to come into my view. Just moments earlier I had used these feathers to send the energy of the tree, the soul companion I know so well, into flight—releasing her soul, to go where she needs to go, to help another as she has helped me, to become an Ancestor of good character.

And here I am begging to get these sacred owl feathers back into my possession. Suddenly, I realize they must be part of the tree's flight. I send gratitude to the feathers and accept their loss to me. They must be needed elsewhere. Releasing them, I sit back down to meditate on the lessons and gifts of the day, the reciprocity of giving and receiving. As I rise to gather all the items and return to the house, I am surprised to discover the owl feathers, once again, lying upon the rock. Filled with joyful gratitude, I understand I had to let them go in order to see them once again. Even in death you are my teacher, dear Tree of Many Voices.

"Ho Ma-doh! Huge Gratitude!"

The heavenly dream to reconnect the plant world to the human one,
aware, awakens conscious forces, capable of liberating,

reuniting the planet to the divine whole…
for a cosmic signal which brings humans and plants

on a common planetary path,

happy, aware and evolved…

🖋 Oberto Airaudi, "Falco"

Maple Tree

by Mariénne Kreitlow

She calls, "Come muss me up. Jostle me."

The wind probes her robe.

She rustles like a papery tambourine.

The veins in her leaves as strong as supple bone,

anchoring webs of seamless green.

(She will not give one up.

Not in summer's heat, unless broken by storm.)

How would it be to lift my skirt and house a hundred birds?

To flow with sap inside so many limbs?

To clothe myself in shadow, reaching for the light?

Oledas
The Ancient Ones

by R.Maya Briel

illustrated by P. Cleve Ragan

There are trees that live in the Gobi Desert, in Mongolia. They stand and tell a story of another time and place. Back when western Mongolia was not yet a desert, and the Chinese had not destroyed the many monasteries built atop the underground rivers. Back when the "sweet water" rivers still flowed above the ground.

In this ancient time, there was a monk of no import. He had traveled long, searching for his place. Everywhere he looked, he was surrounded by a dying land—yet this place drew him. It was a place to bring new life and love. The nothingness touched his heart; a canvas so wide and free. It was a place of unending cycle.

The monk's heart yearned for more, as he placed each Joshua tree seedling carefully in the sun-baked ground. His knapsack had carried these seedlings from an old way of existence. He nurtured them, and prayed that they would survive in the stress-hardened soil. Always, he tended the Joshua tree saplings—spending his days in the hot sun, carrying water to each of their root balls. Often he would talk with them, as he cared for their leaves and bark and roots, encouraging them to not give up. To throw away the stresses of life is to throw away life itself. Feeding upon the love which the man carried in his heart for them, the young trees grew strong, even as the monk wizened and grew less agile. Still, he bent to tend them day after day. They were family, each a part of the other.

There came a time when the trees gave as much as they took from the old monk. They now shaded his path from the intensity of the sun. The trees could not ease the labor from his steps, but they learned how to draw life to themselves, much as the old monk had done for them. The birds stopped to rest among the branches, the droppings and leaves and insects strengthened the soil, and the deep underground water was drawn to their roots. The trees now had the ability to attract their own life force. To bring creation as an earth unto themselves. Travelers began seeking rest in this growing oasis.

Listening deeply into his heart-connection with his trees, the old monk heard a healing flow deep within this growing web of life. The trees' strength seemed to ease the stress and illness of others under the tutelage of the old one's gentle hands. His blended ministering of heart and love and connection drew those with weakness and need to the area. Many also came to learn and listen to the trees. "Don't let any 'bad happening' be enough to destroy your spirit, or your connection to the web of life within each of you. Allow your strength to take the hand of your weakness and walk together, each in acceptance of the other." Those who came seeking purity of heart, healed. Those who held tightly, and were served by their weaknesses, did not.

The old one, with failing eyes and softer breath, knew that his time was ending. He grieved the time when he would no longer be able to listen and walk among his tree friends. His heart pounded with the ache of being separated from his life's blood flowing in the ancient trees. Yet he recognized the wisdom of the cycle of Life and Death, and as he lay down within the shadow of his planted tree of life, he pledged that he would one day return to these dear ones. It was a pledge torn from his heart, and held by the wind in the branches of the trees.

1997

As we bumped along in the small, exceedingly hot unair-conditioned bus, I pulled the fabric of my high tech wick-away shorts from the sticky seat. Our bread, the only remaining food, was moldy from a week of intense heat. And the drivers were a bit hung-over from celebrating the end of a very unusual tourist trip. It was high noon in the Gobi Desert.

I began to feel my heartbeat thumping strongly in my chest. Surely it was from the heat? I took a couple swallows of warm water, and poured more over my head, sopping it up with my bandana. I felt a yearning deep in my heart. The hot air was hard to breathe. I tied the damp bandana across my nose and mouth. The yearning grew uncomfortable in my chest. For what? A sadness began to haunt me, and yet, I could feel waves of love flowing up from the desert beyond. A deep, deep loving, beyond anything I had ever experienced. What? What? I stood impatiently in the bouncing bus wondering, waiting. "Your life's blood flows in us." I looked around the bus, yet no one was addressing me. Again, I heard them. "Your life's blood flows in us. You have honored your pledge to one day return." It was then that I saw them out in the distance.

The trees the Mongols call "Oledas" stood out like beacons, tall in the shifting sands and rock. They were calling to me. I could actually feel them across the distance. My heart tightened with intensity from a heavy, thick unfurling love that survives throughout the ages of time. I needed desperately to get out of that bus. Tears ran from my eyes, as I felt and imagined the strength of a love, a devotion, a pledge of that enduring gift. The words were pounding in my head, wave after wave, "My life's blood flows in those trees...My life's blood flows in those trees." The moment we stopped moving, I rushed from the bus with that love tightening, yet bursting in my chest.

Five trees remained. They were incredibly strong to weather this desert. Overwhelmed, I walked to the closest of them, and I looked down and saw the "tree of life" form, as a shadow upon the ground. I was stunned as it resonated with the tree of life within my own body. My arms and legs, my whole body vibrated with love and life "beyond time." My arms went around the nearby tree, and I soaked up the feelings of acceptance and love and surety of a pledge satisfied, so deep in my bones. I dropped to my knees within the shadow of that ancient tree and watered it one last time. Full Circle.

Stillness of mountains,
cold rain on barren branches
in a drifting fog.

    🖋 Calen Rayne

Mist on horizon,
oak trees rise from jagged peaks,
dew on their branches.

    🖋 Calen Rayne

Stay

by Larry Winters

Before you finish your tea

Tell me again how the sun tangled in the trees

The part about the lone black bird landing in your heart

It made me shiver inside

When you placed your finger near your eye

And told me if I looked into your pupil

I'd see all the souls of dead trees

gathered in the craters on the moon.

I'll make another pot, stay.

T. Manes

Tree Hugging Cactus

by Gurutej

illustrated by Thomas E. Manes

This is both a very simple and very complex story. My daughter was in the hospital at the Mayo Clinic in Scottsdale, AZ. Great hospital, challenging situation. The clinic has this wonderful sculptural cactus garden, with a beautiful bronze statue of a shamaness changing into an eagle. There were many varieties of lovely and rare cacti. A little waterfall was my meditation place, while my daughter was having her surgeries.

This garden was our haven. It was our refuge. My beloved partner, Keith, and I, would come out and do walking meditations, barefoot on the warm cement, in order to ground ourselves. On most days, during our break we did yoga, as well. We looked at every cactus plant in the garden, admiring each one. On every visit, we noticed new plants, or revisited the ones we really loved, or were amazed by some tiny ones, that we would "awww" over.

There was so much pain in the hospital. Yet, so much hope and life in the garden. That is what we gathered to bring back into the room with us. One day I took pictures to show my daughter, whose greatest desire was to "get out" and walk outside—really to run, but walking would do. She did not want to be swallowed up by the hospital. At the time she got sick, she was in medical school, preparing for a career in hospitals. Even so, she had always come out of her hospital stays sicker than when she went in. This photo shoot was after she had been in the hospital for about six weeks. I knew what she meant about getting outside, because coming out to this cacti oasis, almost every day, was one of the things that kept us on track.

One day, a brilliant realization came near the end of our stay at the Mayo. As I was taking pictures, I looked up and noticed something truly spectacular, which we had never noticed before. This mesquite tree was hugging a saguaro cactus. Actually, two different mesquite trees were hugging two different saguaro cacti. There was a burly saguaro cactus which had been placed, perhaps, too close to this mesquite tree—so the tree just did what trees can do. It stretched it's beautiful branched arms, and encompassed the burly saguaro. The mesquite was actually hugging the saguaro cactus!

As I snapped pictures of this magical tree, it spoke to us. It said that however thorny this journey had been, and continues to be, embrace it. Spread the branches of your arms and hug all parts of this blisteringly challenging situation. If this tree can hug a cactus, could I totally "hug" the thorniness of our current situation? Could I, now, see the wonder of this entire journey, and the grace and love of this amazing soul, my daughter?

She is that love. Her mantra was always, "I want to be here as long as I can still experience love and gratitude." She was the essence of innocence, love, grace, and gratitude—in situations most would scream through. She, like this wondrous mesquite tree, had to wrap her arms around the thorniest of all cacti: death. We each had to become like that tree, and embrace the Will of the Divine.

Breathe the Wind Through Your Skin

by Shiila Safer

Daydreaming
free-flowing
structure-free
breezy and full of song
I call to your soul
to release worry and concern
and feel the freedom
in this moment
perched as you are
in the heart of the tree
daily tasks fall away
in a timeless space
marked by the sun in the sky
and the birds singing in your ear

Breathe the wind
through your skin
every cell opening to take it in
more than feeling it
is breathing it
How porous can you be?

What wisdom is being blown on the wind?
From what part of the world?

Every pore opens to receive
like a sponge
my edges are not so hard
more like a living organism
passing information
across a thin cell wall

I am not so solid as I like to think
when I loosen the notion
of the boundary of my skin
separating my body from the outside world
and feel the space in between the molecules
and the breeze flowing through
my arms and then my chest and face
permeable, accessible
I open to being the energy body
that is touched by everything
riding on the air

I feel BIGGER
and full of energy
filled with information
beyond words
out of the mental body
and into my physical and energetic body
with greater access
to Universal truths
and Earth wisdom

the briefest vision of faces
of the Ancestors, spirits
shimmering into existence
for a nano-second
becoming one, then the other
before my Inner Eye
reminding me that I am not alone
beautiful faces
gentle loving faces
melt into my own

consciously I choose to feel my skin
as a boundary again
in preparation for returning
to my every day world of activities
yet it's not the same
as it was before
there is more spaciousness
inside my being
and I bring that gift
into the world with me

Lilac's Lessons

by Carol Bennington

illustrated by Karen Wecker

It was springtime in Santa Fe, New Mexico. I found myself drawn to the herb garden, where the lilac was in full bloom. The beautiful clusters of tiny light purple blossoms and their aroma filled my senses, and delighted my heart. This heavenly scent beaconed me to sit beneath the branches, and inhale the fragrance. With each breath, I was transported to my previous connections with lilac.

Lilac took me deep into my roots, because she is one of the links to my ancestors. I mentally flashed back to my first lilac connection. It was with my favorite grandmother, who represented unconditional love for me. Grandma would always have huge bouquets of lilacs around my birthday time. Her house was surrounded by the lilacs planted by my great-grandparents. For more than a century, these thick flowering trees have spread to create a long fencerow. With each move, as an adult, I would go back to the family farm, and get new shoots to plant at my new home. However, I did not bring lilacs after my most recent move, because they would not survive in the desert climate of Phoenix, Arizona.

In Santa Fe, with lilac's nurturing presence, my grief surfaced. I hadn't really denied my grief, but I had not attended to myself at the level that matched my needs. Lilac whispered that it was time to own the depth of my sorrow, over being exiled from my green companions of the Great Lakes region to the desert, where I was a stranger to most plants. Lilac invited me to be present, acknowledge my grief, and to let go.

Much to my surprise, it was Lilac who initiated this reunion, rather than myself. This bittersweet time was a powerful teaching tool. Lilac held gentle space for me to grieve, and to let go. This sacred time of being with lilac was a reunion with my connection to lilac, and with myself.

While in the presence of the Santa Fe lilac, I knew I needed to find a lilac flower essence to continue being in relationship with lilac, when I returned home. Flower essences, also known as flower remedies, work energetically to balance emotional disharmonies. Each flower corresponds with a range of specific emotions. Lilac flower essence is about letting go, and realizing when we have completed some aspect of our lives. My lilac flower essence experience replicated my experience with the Santa Fe lilac. While I couldn't take the Santa Fe lilac home, I could keep an essence with me, as a flower remedy, to provide nurturing support.

I would return to the Santa Fe lilac in memory, to experience the reunion with her presence and wisdom. Lilac had become my coach and cheerleader as she helped me recognize my grief, and supported moving through it. She encouraged me to 'just let go' as she chanted, "you can do it, and all is well."

Lilac was a bridge from my past into the present; while letting go, lilac helped me claim the treasures of my past. Reconnecting with lilac on a deeper level assisted me in a growing relationship with all aspects of nature. While her central message was about my need to let go of what no longer served me, her nurturance was also about connecting and growing deeper. Lilac's aroma is about remembering, and for me it was about remembering my very deep connection with plants. This epiphany's focus was about my ability to be intimate with plants.

The lessons resulting from a few days with the Santa Fe lilac changed the course of my life. It redirected the focus of my doctoral dissertation. More importantly, I changed as a result of this experience, and so did the trajectory of my path. As they say, when the student is ready, the teacher appears: it was lilac who initiated our reunion and guided this adventure. I remain grateful for the beauty, fragrance, essence, wisdom and lessons of lilac.

Falling Leaves

by Ashe Godfrey

I live near Perth Australia in the beautiful hillside Forrest of Jarrahdale. I wrote this poem a few years ago during a time of much frustration and despair about the uncontrollable logging taking place in old growth forests not only in our SouthWest but globally. What a sight it would be if the trees could fight back.

The pieces aren't fitting together
Watch the dead leaves fall
Allow new things to grow
Let the trees grow tall
Shadows give off an illusion
Things that really aren't there
Let the dead leaves fall
Depart without a care
Slumber is upon us
Close our eyelids tight
Dream the trees grow stronger
Won't give up without a fight
We are the trees
Try to grow strong
We are the leaves
Try to hold on
When we have died
Fall to the ground
Try to let go
But not without sound

Sentinel Inviting: My Wise Friend

by Sheila Armitage

illustrated by Thomas E. Manes

Let me introduce you to my friend.

Her name is Sentinel Inviting.

We met eight years ago on the first day I drove by. I had not met anyone like her before, and she was mesmerizing. Since then, we have become firm friends, visiting with one another regularly. I want you to know Sentinel Inviting, because she is wise and welcomes your spirit. I suspect that you will enjoy her.

With majesty, she reigns over the entrance to our land, her sentinel presence beckoning travelers around a large curve that finally delivers them onto a small tract of sacred peaceful nature extending down to a clear, sparkling, singing creek.

"Welcome. You are going the right way," she says as she greets each person who passes by. In fact, everyone must pass by her to get to our house. Sometimes I will take friends back up our drive to see her, since she is a living beauty.

Sentinel Inviting stands beside our drive as it turns left at the bottom of a boulder-strewn hill. Fitted amid the dappled shades of the rocky cliff, I admire her rich bark and green undulating leaves. Her limbs are as large as trees themselves—some are fifteen inches in diameter! Branching out across soil, rocks and asphalt, she reaches out to us on our daily journey.

"Sentinel Inviting" is the overall feeling I receive from her. Emanating female energy: patient, wise, resilient, and loving. There are days we visit in silence, and there are days we chat about life. It is comforting to have this level of intimacy with anyone.

She is a Quercus marilandica Muenchh. Blackjack Oak, Barren Oak, Black Oak, Jack Oak. From the red oak family, she shares some white oak characteristics—she connects across boundaries.

Her Latin name sounds like a spell, and indeed, she has bewitched me as a lifelong friend.

At forty feet tall, she comes from a family of small to medium-sized oaks. At five-foot-two inches, I seem very small standing beside her towering trunk and branches. I am prompted to stretch my torso up, add space between my ribs, allow the slouching and compression to leave my body, and gain half an inch in height. My yoga teacher would be proud.

With bristle-lobed leaves that are shiny on top, and spread with rusty-yellow hair beneath, she stands with distinction in a grove of Live Oaks, coexisting peacefully. Clearly from a different species, she is not afraid to command her own space and be seen.

In autumn, her leaves turn scarlet red, performing in concert with our seasonal Texas sunsets. The western light gleams from behind, sending the sun's illuminated rays through her canopy onto all those fortunate enough to pass by, and experience her glory.

Winter arrives, and as her leaf mantle turns a chestnut brown, brisk winds send the blades somersaulting onto the ground to form a carpet of nourishment over the soil, composting over time.

In spring, hairy catkins announce reentry into the full dress of her summer cloak. Their pink-tinged fringe foretell the beauty of her leathery, deep green, shiny, three-lobed leaves with prominent veins, curving gracefully towards a hairy point. There are no hard edges on this tree.

Sentinel Inviting has soul. Her stocky, gray trunk divides into many dense contorted limbs, with thick dark bark furrowed in deep rectangular plates. Like a crone with gnarled arms, hands, and fingers, she reaches toward the sky.

She is comfortable allowing one to read her face with its lines and wrinkles, gained through a deep-rooted life, which reveals little of her story and experiences.

Apparently, she is slow-growing and short-lived. I would guess Sentinel Inviting to be approximately fifty years old, with a trunk diameter of twenty-eight inches, or so. We are a similar age.

This species of Blackjack Oak forms the "Cross Timbers" in Texas and Oklahoma, which is a forested border of small trees transitioning the area into prairie grassland. Indeed, she also marks the divide between rocky cliffs and grasslands on our land. These trees play a valuable role for both humans and wildlife in their natural habitat: transition trees, marking pathways, and environmental support with their understated strength.

During the long drought in Central Texas, marking our arrival into the twenty-first century, Sentinel Inviting began speaking to me.

"I'm dying," she told me back in the summer of 2010.

"Your roots are deep, and we live by a creek," I replied. "Dig deeper." Not comprehending what she was telling me. The next week she dropped a limb fifteen inches in diameter, a tree in and of itself. My heart sank.

"Let me bring a hose to you," I said.

"That will not bring me enough water, dear. I have been needing water for several years, and I just cannot hang on anymore. We are going into a more severe drought, mark my words. I can feel it. I need to take action now to withstand any chance of surviving."

From September 1, 2010, to November 23, 2011, our acreage received less than an inch of rain, in total. Sentinel Inviting knew this before we humans did.

In fall 2011, she dropped another branch, this time not as large. The rains came the week of Thanksgiving. Praise the heavens! It persisted until spring of 2012, but, due to seven previous years of drought, did not catch-up to normal rainfall levels in Central Texas.

In summer 2012, Sentinel Inviting dropped another branch. "I am preparing myself again," she announced. "The winds have shifted. More drought is coming." Since summer 2012, our microclimate has delivered less than an inch of total rainfall. Once again, Sentinel Inviting foretold the weather.

My heart hurts when she gives up a part of herself. I know I cannot provide enough water for her roots. I have to trust that this wise old tree knows what she needs to do. I shower her with love. I have developed a new practice of beaming out love to the land and trees, as I drive by, hoping that my energy will nourish them.

We have built a new hay barn near her corner. Another possible consequence of our local drought is fire. In this way we can keep the fire hazard of hay away from sources of fuel, such as trees and living structures.

An interesting thing has happened. Two of my horses, and my donkey, cluster near her daily, keeping her company, and sending out their natural healing energy. Three dogs also lie close by almost every day, even in the rain and cold. A tarantula has been spotted near her. A six-foot long Rat Snake extended itself, one day, like a very wobbly "energy vibration line," across our drive from one of her boulders. The snake formed a barrier and would not let me pass by in my car. After waiting for a while, I stepped out and danced on the asphalt, until he slithered away under his boulder, shaded by Sentinel Inviting, issuing an irritated warning fake rattle from his tail.

These sentient beings are her friends, who gather around her regularly. They rest in community, not asking anything of each other, simply happy to share time and space. As I groom my herd by the barn, I make a point to connect with Sentinel Inviting, to chat with her, and send her my love.

It was eight years ago, on Valentine's Day, when I first met Sentinel Inviting. The skies were blue, and the sun beamed through the chilly air. I was very fortunate. My tree friend has taught me to practice...

being fully seen,
stand strong,
dig as deeply as you can,
...and "let go" to survive!

Hoarfrost

by Mariénne Kreitlow

february fog lasting four days
hoarfrost building layer by layer
spiked hairs onto twine
lengthening spears from barb wire
needles stick into stacks on skeletal weeds
daisy head mummies wear hats of white shards
jauntily tipped at precipitous angles
sense the presence of faeries
we walk in their world
see as they see as we follow the lane
our big dog is sucking snow cones off cedars
his greedy mouth guzzles glistening frost
coating his throat a prelude to gin
then clouds crack wide open
pouring out sunlight
trees rain down music
chandeliers shatter and sing out like glass
they fall on our heads crash at our feet
we laugh and we laugh
what was real disappears

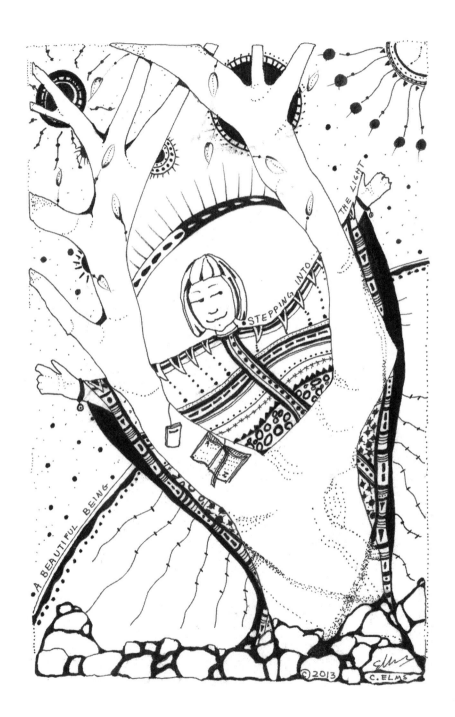

The Climbing Tree

by Peggy Cole
illustrated by Cheryl Elms

We called her "The Climbing Tree." She was just a scrubby, overgrown, multi-branched bush growing near the front of my childhood home. But she had dark shiny leaves that offered a canopy of cooling shade for hot summer days, and a loving nook for each of the neighborhood kids.

We began our association with this tree following our toddler years, when the big adventure was leaping off the front porch into space (which, from an adult perspective, was only about a foot high). Big brave Marty, my older sister by a year, was the first to try putting a foot into a low crook of the tree to hoist herself onto a branch. The power of her perch seemed intoxicating. I had to try it! Soon Patty and Bubba from next door, naughty Mike Robinson from across the street, the five Holland girls who lived at the corner, little Eddie Roberts and the Treadwell sisters were all taking turns climbing onto that first limb.

The tree lured us higher and higher among her branches, rewarding our bravery with the security of more and more comfortable crooks and nooks. Soon there was a favorite spot for each of us. Kids would arrive in our yard shouting "The Climbing Tree!" All would run into her arms. Bringing books and pillows, we spent both social and solitary hours there.

The Climbing Tree was a like a nanny with broad gentle arms, and a love of adventure. We felt she would never hurt us, while instilling the confidence to climb higher and higher as she grew taller and taller. Finally, we were able to climb onto the roof of the little bungalow that had her back. I think it was naughty Mike Robinson's idea to run across that roof, leap down onto the nearby garage roof, and then jump! This display was a huge badge of courage…until the day little Eddie Roberts (who was a bit of a "crybaby") landed wrong, twisted his knee, and hobbled home in tears. We were all busted! Eddie's outraged parents insisted The Climbing Tree was a neighborhood hazard, and should be cut down.

"NO!!!" we screamed. But Daddy agreed to do the awful deed. Marty and I climbed back into our tree's loving embrace with tears of terror, thinking we had provoked her death sentence. We hugged her smooth branches, shaking with our sobs. Although we pleaded with Daddy to let her live, he said perhaps the Roberts were right, and other kids would be hurt if we kept that tree.

Daddy did not get around to cutting down the tree that weekend, nor the next. Eddie Roberts no longer played as much with the bigger kids, so the rest of us quietly resumed our love affair with The Climbing Tree. Perhaps we were getting too big for those uppermost branches to support us, or maybe it was guilt, and fear of losing our sacred place, but it seemed as if the tree simply disallowed us to ever climb onto the roof again.

A year later, just before I entered fourth grade, we moved away, leaving our loving tree behind to invite the next set of neighborhood children to snuggle high into the comfort and culture of her branches.

It was forty-five years later that the spirit of The Climbing Tree, again, appeared in my life. I'd left my marriage wounded and afraid. A friend offered an ailing cottage located on some investment land she owned, and there I took refuge for two years. Towering over and engulfing this cottage was an ancient oak, with the same nurturing spirit as the The Climbing Tree of my childhood. I believed the tree was an angel placed on this earth to heal those who sought her magic, and that I was neither the first, nor the last, to find healing. My relationship with her was very personal and special.

Dark clouds roiled above, as I left my beautiful home to move into this abandoned cottage that January. Even so, wonderful supportive friends came to help. We painted the rooms with colorful faux finishes, and got the shower working again. I learned how to gather soil and sawdust for the composting toilet, and acquired a hot plate and heater from thrift shops. Thankfully, my beloved dog, who seemed as confused and upset about the breakup as I, came with me.

My sacred contract of marriage was broken along with my heart. With finances in ruin and crushed esteem, my beautiful home and property were traded in for this mysterious alternative lifestyle. I had done my best, giving away my love, my money, and my power. I had been betrayed by my husband and a friend, and felt trampled and abandoned.

Now, alone with my dog, questions raged in my head over what went wrong. I sat in the cold tiny shack without proper plumbing or electricity, and poured out my sorrows on its great embracing oak. I called her "Grandmother Oak."

"Get up!" I heard her say, "This is Your Time. Quit wallowing in your pain and welcome yourself back into your immense love." I was dumbfounded. I had no love at all for this "me" who had walked out on her marriage, was hopelessly in debt, and aching for her lost land.

"Release it!" she snapped. "Find the good in where you are. Then perhaps you can begin to find the good in who you are." I put on my coat, and walked outside to touch her ragged trunk.

"Are you really talking to me, or am I going a little nuts?"

"No nuts, only acorns." I could feel her grinning back at me.

I leaned against her and sighed, "Who am I and what am I doing here?"

"A beautiful being stepping into the light," she whispered.

"But how can I grin up at the sun through these dark clouds?" I moaned. "I will start with you, Grandmother. Your beauty is in your age, your size and your wrinkles and scars, yet those are the same qualities he said made me undesirable. But I find you amazing in both your inner and outer beauty."

"Yes!" she smiled, "I can feel your distress lifting. Now every day you must find what there is to appreciate. Welcome your darkness. Explore it without fear. Your shadow can be your friend and teacher. Take some time to sit in your shade, but always, always find something to appreciate."

And so it began, this internal dialog with a magnificent tree, and this quest to know and love myself. I realized that I had permitted the strength and leadership of big sister Marty, girlfriends and boyfriends, husband, bosses, (and really anyone) to direct my actions, and have their way with my life. I had never been alone to make my own decisions. I did not even know what I liked and did not like—until losing it all and "finding myself" in this lonesome cabin.

I became Grandmother Oak's handmaiden. I gathered just the right stones for a medicine wheel around her base. I purified her with sage and sweet grass, and conducted ceremonies in which she participated with sweet indulgence. In turn, she drew in the four winds, with which she had an abiding relationship. I consulted experts for her health, spread sacred manure, and plucked as much of her ball moss as possible. Mostly I just loved her, absorbed her nurturing energy, and sat at her feet accompanied by my woes.

She listened. I climbed into her arms, and dried my tears with her leaves. She summoned the owls to sit in her branches, and dialog with me. When the weather was bad, she was right outside my kitchen window. When the weather was pleasant, I settled in her lap with a pillow and a book. In the spring, I hung a swing from a branch, and she dipped toward the earth to hold me. I spent many hours just swinging and listening to her soothing sounds.

Grandmother Oak motivated me to find my strength. I found it through gratitude and appreciation. I hung mirrors and portraits of myself in the house. I conversed with the light and the dark within me, until the lines blurred and the labels dropped away. I was learning to accept myself. As I walked the land surrounding the cottage, I fell in love with it, but without the attachment that held me captive at my previous home. This appreciation "game" put a spring in my step, and love into the photographs I made of my retreat haven.

Grandmother Oak also heartened me to find my bend. I had been in uncomfortable negotiations with my ex. Family and friends, who were fiercely protective, urged me to get what I deserved, be firm in my stance, even get revenge. Then, one day, a big storm began brewing in the sky. When it hit during the night, I heard a resounding "crack," and joined the dog in fretting about everyone's safety. Early morning light revealed a large branch, torn away by fierce winds, lay dying on the ground. Grandmother Oak asked me to walk the land and take note of what other branches might be down. On my ramble, I learned that strength was not rigidity, but the ability to yield and bend—sidestepping a force hurled without particular target or malice. As a result, the example, set by broken limbs in a severe storm, saved the friendship which wished to endure a bad marriage.

Grandmother Oak knew she had accomplished her mission when I came back from one of my walks, grinning from ear to ear.

"Grandmother!" I beamed, "I have found my best friend! She likes all the things that I like, she walks the same fast pace as I do, she has the same boundless curiosity. And guess what? She IS me!"

It was not long after I left, that I heard another had secured the refuge of this little cottage which I had come to view as a sacred sanctuary, along with the love of wonderful Grandmother Oak. Healed and happy, I moved out to complete the task of making my peace, selling my land and home, and indulging myself in a long, loving goodbye.

Grandmother Oak nurtured her new family with the same joy I had experienced. Sometimes, when I go there to visit, my eyes fill with tears the moment I touch her ancient trunk. I feel we will always be connected—our roots share the Earth from which we both give and receive nourishment and love—and that unites us, in some way, forever.

Clear Tree

by Shiila Safer

I can see myself standing tall
and energy flowing freely through me like the trunk of a tree
both up from the Earth through the roots
and down from the sky through the branches
through the clear trunk
without obstruction or blockages
open
clear
spacious
stillness
Clear Tree

The Trees & Me

by Lynne Russell

illustrated by Kerri Hummingbird Lawnsby

Once the smoke and the evacuation ban lifted, reality began to set in. News people called it the worst fire in Texas history. Emergency people called it the perfect fire. All conditions were indeed perfect for uncontrollable devastation. Seventeen hundred homes, and 95% of the Lost Pines of Bastrop State Park were destroyed. My dream home and five acres of the precious Loblolly Pines of Bastrop were spared. The fire stopped about 100 yards up the hill from my house.

The fire blazed through our county in September 2011, a year and a half ago. After the initial upheaval, things have continued to change around here. According to utility hook-up records, about half of the homes are being rebuilt. There are lots of trucks. I'd never heard of Buc-ee's, until they built a huge one at the main intersection in Bastrop. I wonder if anyone else remembers the acreage of happy unburned pine trees that was mowed down to build the parking lot for that place?

Opportunities for volunteerism abound, especially tree planting on private properties and in the park. Millions of Loblolly saplings will be planted over the next five years by volunteers and contract labor. I suspect that planting trees makes people feel good, and I'm glad volunteers are getting to do some of the work. The story "Loblolly seeds saved in time for new forest" in the Houston Chronicle helps me believe in miracles.

I'm a better person since the fire. I'm a better helper. I'm a better friend. I think I'm braver, too. I had to drive through fire (actually smoke, but it could've been fire) to evacuate. I've enjoyed telling that part of my story. I've learned a lot about myself by dealing with some feelings never experienced before this fire. For example, there's the guilt of being spared, coupled with the fear of not being spared the next time. Relaxing is getting easier. Especially among the trees. The trees and I are grateful to be alive and committed to being right here, right now. How I got to that point is my story...my story about my connection with my trees. It's a conversation. What did it take to get the conversation going? I had to ask for advice. But first I had to realize I needed help.

Several weeks after the fire, I was feeling a myriad of emotions. Gratitude, of course. Thank goodness I know about the power of gratitude, and the need to get to the lesson as soon as I can. There's always a lesson. This one started out as "nothing is permanent." That's the last thing I wrote in my journal the morning of the fire. It didn't take long for me to realize I should keep my gratitude and my lessons to myself. No one who has just lost everything wants to hear about my gratitude or what I've learned.

Along with the gratitude was the sadness I felt every time I left my home and precious forest. The burnt trees and homes were evident for miles along the roads I drove daily. The sadness of the stories weighed heavily. The stories could be heard everywhere—grocery lines, teachers' lounges, birthday parties. The pictures of lost animals at the convenience stores grabbed my heart. (I found out later that the animal control people returned nearly 200 dogs to their owners.) I didn't know what to do with the sadness. So I stuffed it. For some reason I thought I had to be strong or calm or collected—something other than the emotional basket case I felt inside.

And then I began to feel deep guilt, the emotion I do best. (If you know anything about being NF on the MBTI, you will know what I mean.) 'Survivor's Guilt' got to be a popular term to explain an unusual desire to help others. Helping was everywhere. Some helpful. Some not. Everybody had a story. I decided the best thing I could do at that time was be a good listener and offer support.

Back when 2011 began, I had made a resolution to face some of my fears. I made a list of possibilities and 'Fear of losing everything by fire' was not one of them. Denial is an amazing thing. I live at the end of a cul-de-sac in a pine forest. Was I prepared for possible evacuation? No. I had no idea what to take besides my dogs, laptop and good hat. (Now I know to take clean underwear and a power cord.) Did I pay attention to the commotion on the street created by neighbors getting out? No. I stayed curled up in the air-conditioned Airstream thinking I'll find out soon enough. Duh. I sure did. My friend in town called to see if I had evacuated, and that's when I found out I was on my own. Denial and inner guidance kept me calm, and eventually safe with friends in Elgin, away from the fire. So the fear of losing everything by fire didn't set in until I returned home. I was afraid to be at home. Afraid to be in the forest. Afraid to have to deal with all the loss, if it happened to me. I had lost my connection with the trees and my beautiful place. Practicing gratitude while I worried about loss was disconcerting. I no longer found comfort among the trees.

It was that feeling of disconnection from the trees that led me to a session with Shiila Safer, a nature-based mentor and coach, and one of my WooWoo Women friends. The shift in my state of mind was profound. She helped me connect with the trees in a way I didn't know was possible. This is what I wrote in my journal the next morning: "I loved my session with Shiila yesterday, about grounding and connecting with the trees. Communicate with them. Establish a relationship. Share the joy of living with them. We are all one with the earth. Celebrate the connection."

In one of Shiila's exercises I received this message from the trees. "Share the joy of living. We know you care. Don't be afraid. Be aware. Be there. Be here. Right now." Cool, huh? Anyway, I felt a thousand times better. Just talking to someone about my relationship with my trees was a great relief. It's not something I was comfortable sharing with many people.

I loved the notion that I could actually communicate with these trees. I've talked to trees for years. Expressed my love and appreciation but never conversed. I think actual conversation is hard to come by, and the idea that I could be conversing right here in my own yard was really cool. I wondered how it might get started. A couple of days later I found myself sitting on my Tree Deck, wondering what I was going to do next. So I asked the trees what I should do. The message I got was to be grateful to be alive. They were glad to be alive, and I should be, too. And that I should relax and lighten up. Tears finally came. The relief was amazing. Right then and there, I committed to being here as long as the trees are here. I got the feeling that we could work on our relationship and learn to communicate. What a hoot. I may be going off my own little deep-end here, but I'm thinking that communicating with trees is gonna be a lot easier than communicating with either of my husbands.

That's the story of how I got to the point when I could say, "I am grateful to be alive and I am committed to being right here, right now." Two days after my session with Shiila, I heard Dr. Will Taegel talk about communicating with Nature. And the next month, Shambhala Sun published an article by David Abram entitled "The Living Language."

"Language is not a uniquely human possession," he writes.

The earth speaks through us. Meaning comes from the ongoing interaction and intercourse between oneself and the rest of the earthly cosmos. This notion that I can converse with the trees, and even develop a relationship with them thrilled me. And now I had validation from 'expert' sources.

Epilogue

Relaxing continues to be a daily practice. I'm glad I am committed to writing morning pages. My conversations with the trees come to me through my journaling. Asking, "what do I do next?" has rendered very helpful advice. "Keep communicating with the people who really like you," and "Keep the conversations going," have given me a basis for many of my relationships.

I seldom ask anyone for advice, much less follow advice that is freely given. I don't like being told what to do. But my trees are a different matter. The advice is so clear and to the point, that it's hard to resist, even for me.

Communication is my thing, and successful aging has been my quest for 30 years. Now that I am that happy old person I worked hard to become, I am amazed that conversing with trees is a highlight of my day. The notion that I can commune with the trees and ask them for advice tickles me. I have no other elders. Listening was the gift I gave my dad in his old age. He loved it. I suspect the trees do, too. I know I do.

Night Womb

by Mariénne Kreitlow
illustrated by Dianne Marion

alexandra scaling branches
divining rod
blindly dances
presses muscle into wood
seeks fruit from wood
juice from wood
wine from wood
seeking knot the vines
that wind her toes
and penetrate her ligaments
and bind her
knot seeing she
the skin and elbows
formed by ancient lesions wrapping
wrapping wrapping wrapping
wrapping
and gently hanging her
gently
gently hanging her
as night whispers
she
a lantern
in the dark

Gifts from Trees

pecan

peach

pear

magnolia

Bois d'Arc
horse apple

persimmon

fig

S. Carter

Gifts from Trees
While Growing Up in Texas During the Great Depression

by Martha Knies

illustrated by Sharon Carter

Helen, my slightly older sister, came down crying as she scrambled through the thorny branches as fast as she could. It wasn't very fast, however, because mama blue jay was chasing her and pecking on her skull, now bleeding and dripping onto little Helen's white shirt and striped shorts. She had had the audacity to climb too close to the mama bird's nest of little ones.

This is just one of many memories of my pre-adolescent years...generally delightful years...of climbing, hiding, listening, and planning adventures in that old Bois d'Arc tree in our backyard. The tree still stands, although some limbs are dead, and the tree no longer produces its large fruit which we called "horse-apples." To our knowledge, neither horses nor humans partook of this attractive green ball. Squirrels dug for the little achenes (seeds) buried inside; and quail would eat them, too, if any were around.

This particular tree, also known as Osage Orange, Bodark and Hedge Apple, was well known in pioneer days, because of its hard wood and stout thorns which served several important purposes. Before the invention of barbed wire, these fairly fast growing trees were planted to make impenetrable fences. Even before that, Osage Indians, among others, used the arching branches of this tree to make their bows—hence its French name, Bois d'Arc—which means "bow of the wood." It is said that some early house loans were refused unless the house's wooden piers rested on stumps made from these tree trunks, because the wood was so hard and resistant to decay. I think this was true for the house I lived in, because those house piers were still there when we tore the house down, almost one hundred years after it was built.

Because of its large leaves and its location at the very back of our yard, it made a great hiding place for me and my two sisters. It became our tree house, private and hidden, far enough away from our parents who, we thought, had no idea where we were. This tree overhung an alley, through which walked any number of individuals totally oblivious to our presence in the tree. We would be very, very quiet. Once we overheard a lovers quarrel. Tee hee! Usually, however, only tired workers carrying groceries trekked by on this shortcut home.

In a small niche within the tree we stored our stash of two-to-three inch dried grapevine sticks and matches. Why? To smoke, of course. Bitter as they were, they provided us with that first illicit underage smoking experience. I can remember to this very day when I decided to give up the "habit"—I envisioned myself as a grownup smoking grapevines! No sir, this wasn't going to be my future, so I quit right then and there. And I never smoked again—not even a real, adult cigarette.

Whenever my sisters and I heard sirens screaming, we immediately climbed as high as possible to see if we could detect smoke, or a big blazing fire. Then we dreamed of being firefighters or smoke jumpers or forest rangers.

Yes, climbing the Bois d'Arc, and other trees, was a childhood passion for me, but also then, as a child, I began my adoration of the magnificent, large creamy and fragrant blooms of a magnolia tree. There was one in our neighbor's yard, and she would let me come over and pick a choice blossom, or two, to take to my teachers. I carefully kept any fingers from touching the flower, because I wanted it to be perfect, not covered with brown spots caused by fingerprints. The whole class would admire the bloom's beauty, and the teacher always showed appreciation for this special gift.

After our neighbor died, my brothers and sisters pitched in and bought the property, just so my mother could claim ownership of that magnolia tree. We enjoyed it for years.

My sisters and I also enjoyed the peach, the pear, and the fig trees in our yard. We didn't get to harvest too much fruit from those trees, because the birds and insects wanted them as badly as we did. If we were lucky, Mother could make a couple of peach cobblers, two or three jars of peach and fig preserves, and maybe make a few more from the pear trees. The little native persimmon tree in a neighbor's yard made for quick and tasty bites on the run…if you knew when the persimmons were ripe enough to be sweet—not one day before! Puckered lips were not a good experience! This little tree, now nearly endangered in the state of Texas, still lives in the neighborhood.

Mama required us to walk to the city park on cold, windy days in early fall, when Pecan Trees, the State Tree of Texas, began dropping their rich tasty nuts. We got up early in the morning, before school, and walked at least a half-mile to the park. We knew where every "good" pecan tree was, that is, the trees with the largest paper-shell pecans, not the small hard-shelled native ones. Working as fast as we could, we bent down over and over so we could fill our sacks and get back home. In the evenings, after homework time, we would shell the pecans. If we were lucky, Mama might have a "made-from-scratch" pecan pie for us the next day after school. The thought of a homemade pie, or some oatmeal pecan cookies, made our cold morning hunts worthwhile. These long-life trees still stand in the city park, today.

After Mama planted some pecan trees in our yard, she would often say, "Someday, the pecans from these trees will pay my taxes." Unfortunately, she didn't live long enough to see that day, but her neighbors sure enjoyed coming over and harvesting the pecans for themselves.

Today, some seventy years later, I still love and appreciate trees. I love their shade, their shapes, their flowers, their fragrances, their bark, their stateliness—everything about them. Most of all, I believe it's the childhood memories trees stir up, with the sense of family and secrecy and tastiness and beauty and good times—which still reside in my heart from a long ago little girl's poverty-stricken childhood years.

My parents are gone now; my older sister who was pecked on her scalp as she scrambled down the tree is gone; my other sister and I live in different towns. The house is gone, too. The battered, dying, (and probably bewildered) Bois d'Arc still stands...alone. Not proudly, not lively, not useful. Just as a reminder...when day-dreaming children lived a simple, uncluttered and undistracted childhood. Years of which my own children are unaware; reason enough to record this narrative for those yet to come.

Reflections

by Lillie Rowden

Fruit and flowering shrubs strewing petals,
Soft colors carpeting tender firstborn grass,
Rain clouds hovering, scent of weeping dew,
All the earth created new.

Ancient trees with broken boughs,
Decked in spring's bright hope,
Sheltered with birdsong - concealed, windblown sigh,
Eternity glimpsed in age and rue.

Sing out my heart to the raven's cry -
Awake! And see what is real -
Flashing dark light in dove grey heaven,
Now gently settling out of view.

When storm and shower cleanse the world,
Sudden the rainbow's hue,
Vibrant, glimmering stream gathering the shadowed sky,
Reflecting the light anew.

Tree Love

by Wendy Grace
illustrated by Cheryl Elms

I am always amazed when I go out for a walk and encounter the trees. I leave the house feeling like my usual self, and then I start touching the trees. It is as though a subtle world of interconnection opens. I feel their presence as being far greater than the wood on which I rest my hand. Even as I write, the tree presence comes back to me. I hear dialogs which are not the ones I normally hear. These dialogs carry inspiration, and seem to be connected to a vast field of life beyond the physical.

I have been part of the Damanhur tree orienting project, and it has enabled me to spend many hours with trees. They have changed into living friends. Next to them, I feel profound encouragement for life. They consistently lift and clear my energy and feelings. They pass me messages about trees and about myself. Their touch is always poetic. They sometimes come to me in dreams with messages. At first these communications seemed to be projections of myself...then they expanded to include experiences I would have to put into another category.

I was in New York recently, walking in the park, greeting the trees. When I went near the trees that grew close to where I was born, and where I was pushed along in a baby carriage, I was flooded with memories of childhood. A kind of memory that I do not usually have. Perhaps the trees helped trigger my experience. When I walked beyond that location, the memories stopped flowing. In spiritual traditions, trees are thought to be carriers of memory. I feel many memories have returned and enlarged my relationship with trees.

One of my most precious experiences was when I came upon a group of redwoods. Examining them, I realized they were in a circle which was unusually large for redwood circles—perhaps twenty feet in diameter. My attention was guided to the center where there was a large stump. Out of the stump grew a fragile looking sprout of redwood, and an assortment of branches in strange forms. Immediately, I felt that the surrounding circle was aware of that central stump, and perhaps protecting it. Very few competing shrubs grew inside the circle. I was overcome with an awareness of the subtle body of the old tree that was once there. I experienced it as a huge, very active energetic tree, which supported the trees in the circle. Although most of the wood of the old one was gone, I realized that the being was still alive, connecting and living in the subtle world. It carried a force that was enormous compared to the smaller trees in the circle. From that moment on, I began to spend time with the old ones through their huge ancient stumps—acknowledging and honoring them for all the energy and memories that they still hold and share with the surrounding young ones. I also knew that somehow my experience with them enhanced their energy as they did mine.

For me, it was a strong message about the interconnectedness of life with its present and past forms, and the very real power of ancestry. Later, when I was climbing around a large ancestral stump, I was poked in the side by a stick...and received it as a nudge of affection from the tree world.

Spending so much time with trees has cultivated a profound intimacy that is very different from what I have with my fellow humans. It has helped me reach beyond my human point of view. Through trees, I have come to feel subtly connected to times in the evolution of the planet that predate when humans walked. It is clearly a relationship that grows when I wake from my human trance of business, and enter the world of trees. The trees and I share consciousness, and we nurture each other. With our shared attention—and positive intention—life strengthens and expands. I have come to experience this awakening to interspecies consciousness as actually feeding the aliveness of the field of nature. I am so much more than I believed I was, and nature is so much more than I had ever dreamed. I am grateful to have found this new relationship.

This is some of what I have learned from trees:

When I first started working with trees in depth, I had the experience of trees being a metaphor for my nervous system. Metaphorically and intuitively, I saw them also as an incredibly intricate nervous system for the planet. The way their branches reached up and out into the spaces of the air, the way the roots reached deep into the ground, and the way each species did it differently spoke to me of my own consciousness. Just being with them, I seemed to be learning things about myself. I could sense my own roots reaching into the ground and my own branches reaching into the air...I felt myself as a creature of the earth receiving sustenance from our dear planet, and from the light, and presence of the sun, moon and stars. The wood spoke to me of being a concrete expression of a vast inter-dimensional network that reaches into the subtle realms of life. I intuitively knew that subtle forms of life—consciousness, and even other beings—could come through this inter-dimensional aspect of trees. Opening to this awareness could help all of us to have the possibility to know more fully our greater nature. I realized with an "aha!" moment that the trees were mediators of elements and light energy, contributing to the evolution of life on the surface of this planet.

With these thoughts and intuitions, I felt amazingly alive and invigorated. Running around on the uneven soft surface of the forest, while talking with trees, was healing my body, mind and soul. Tree trunks seemed like individuals standing in an amazing matrix of interconnection of earth, starlight, sunlight, moonlight, air, temperature...an amazing gift of life. Likewise, I felt myself as a human body dancing and moving in the matrix of life, connected with one another by invisible roots reaching down, by invisible branches and leaves reaching upwards...living, dancing, and growing in a spiraling song of life for some purpose beyond the grasp of my comprehension.

"Forest, I want to run through you! Climb your creature trees! Running on your soft earth, my body celebrates your rugged surface! I feel outrageously alive and vital! Life is everywhere around me buzzing with birds and bugs and crusty bark and rot... Mother Redwood, you transport me with your subtle body that reaches out of time into the source of life...you lift my emotions! I remember when I am with you that I am a creature of eternity! I have left behind many stumps and stories in past lives, and I am running free and strong! I am even more resilient knowing you!

Thank you for welcoming me into your community...I come with all aspects of myself, including those parts that I know as I reach beyond my five senses and my ordinary reality...Thank you for sharing your stories and your songs, listening to me, and waking me up to a vast new experience of magical destiny..."

Lighted by the moon, the trees start a song,
they begin an ancient dance, millions of years old…
now the song becomes choral
they orient with aware humans…

 Oberto Airaudi, "Falco"

Connections, encounters, stellar appointments,
to rediscover the mystery, the forgotten, the eternity conquered,
through a concert of happy forests...

 Oberto Airaudi, "Falco"

Secrets of the Trees

by Suzanne McBride

Despite fatigue
I am drawn outside
Into this night
Awash with Light
From a Full Moon
Upon the trees

Live Oak, Tallow, Fruitless Plum
Enfold me amidst St. Augustine
Warm summer night
Moist gentle breeze
Cicadas singing
Leaves dancing
Magic abounding

Silver moonlit sky
Reveals silhouettes of giant beings
Rustling their light-fed joy
Shadows mysterious and deep
Filled with invitation
And promise

Breezes lifting leaves
Gifting movement to those who
Speak clearly through webs of light
I smile, laughing softly
Catching glimpses of the playful joke
Flowing branch to branch and bole to bole

Majesty. Presence. Quiet Joy
The secrets of Life at Night
Offered freely to the Willing

All senses open
I am drawn inside
Into this Light
Made whole with shadows
From the laughing dance
Of trees

Soul Retrieval in the Apple Orchard

by Shiila Safer

illustrated by Sharon Carter

I grab my pillow, journal and pen, and climb the ladder up into Grandmother Oak for my morning writing meditation practice. I sit and connect with her, my inspiration and teacher, and feel the peace flowing through my being. I'm open to the words that want to come through, not knowing where they will take me...

I am told that as soon as I could walk, I would spend my days in the apple orchard behind our country house just south of Paris, France, where I was born. My love for trees was preverbal. I was walking, but not talking, and as the story goes, my Mother could hardly get me to come inside. I only wanted to be with the apple trees. However, I had no conscious memory of this until I was 54 years old, when my husband and I went to France on our honeymoon, coupled with the celebration of our second anniversary.

We stayed in a little B&B in the small town of Nevez, near Carnac on the west coast of France. One morning I stood barefoot under the apple trees in front of the B&B. As I leaned down to pick up an apple and breathed in the orchard's fragrance, I felt a knowing in the cells of my body that I had experienced this before. My whole being relaxed and rejoiced with recognition, while at the same time my awareness was suddenly alert and heightened. I had experienced an identical sudden intensity of feeling only one time before: in a circle of redwoods in northern California. Tears poured from my eyes, and my heart opened. All of this happened in a flash of awareness—a timeless moment in which I was forever changed. It seemed like my cellular structure rearranged itself in the blink of an eye!

I felt whole, in a way which was new for me. "So this is what a soul retrieval is like," I thought to myself. I had become reunited with a part of myself that I had left behind in an apple orchard in France, when we crossed the ocean on a big boat when I was two and a half years old.

I felt gratitude toward the apple trees for this gift of friendship and resonance as a toddler in France, and then again as an adult returning to my homeland so many years later. Gratitude to the apple trees for awakening deep memories inside of me. Tears flow even now as I touch that little girl who never wanted to leave her friends, the apple trees, and her part of the Earth with which she resonated so deeply.

I am reminded of my grandson when he was a one-year-old boy, joyfully walking barefoot in our garden and saying, "Thank you, thank you, thank you," in his little sing-song voice, as he walked by the beets, carrots, lettuce and spinach. I was overjoyed as I watched him, and now I realize why. I recognized, at a deep level, the resonance with him and the plants, as it was with myself at that age with the trees—humans at one with their Mother the Earth.

I feel the separation of the little girl inside me from her tree family and friends. She cried and cried for months when she found herself in New York City (a completely alien ecology, and a far cry from her friendly apple orchard). Nothing would console her. My Mother told me she thought I would never recover. I told her I never had—until I had my experience of reunion with this part of myself and the French apple trees; a step towards recovery after all!

This life-changing moment came when I least expected it. I felt at home with the trees on the part of the Earth that I call "home"—my place of birth. I had been welcomed back! Initiated into an instantly intimate relationship with the apple trees, a reunion of old friends, distant cousins of "Grandmother Oak," connected by their root system in a way that defies linear time and space, and boggles my rational mind. The gift of that experience is a sense of wholeness on a cellular level, reminding me that I am a part of the big picture of life itself. Reminding me of my interconnection with trees and other living things all around me.

As I am writing this story, I am sitting in the lap of Grandmother, a live oak tree which lives in front of our house in Texas. I believe that she also awakens my memories and, in her gentle way, assists with the flow of energy throughout this story. Judging by my tears as the words pour out, I'd say this story wants to be told.

A celestial dance, alive,
to tie and unite ancient brotherhoods
between humans and trees,
with covenants made to reach souls and stars…

🖋 Oberto Airaudi, "Falco"

The Secret Language of Leaves

by Bruce P. Grether

Who would have thought?
With meaning…
The Secret Language of Leaves—
would prove to be so fraught…
That from this field of endeavor—
chased by the Merry Little Breeze
I should be gleaning
All that I have ever been taught—
By trees.

Observer Tree in Tasmanian Forest

by Miranda Gibson

illustrated by Kerri Hummingbird Lawnsby

I did not want to fall in love. Not with this forest and not with this tree. The last time my feet touched the ground, over a year ago now, I stood at the base of this giant, and looked along the tall trunk and into the branches above. I attached myself to a rope and began the 60-meter climb, leaving the moss-soaked forest floor behind as I made my way up along side the tree's great weight. I did so with a knot in my heart, not because of the uncertainty of how long it would be before I returned to the earth, but because I was afraid of falling. Not in the sense of plummeting from a 60-meter height—I'd been climbing trees long enough to know how to keep myself safe from that. But did I know enough about trees to keep my heart safe? I knew I had to be very careful... I couldn't afford to fall in love up here. I'd made that mistake before.

Memories overwhelm me...they open my heart to what it meant to be connected to a place. These memories take me back to a tree called "Old Frontie"—a majestic giant eucalyptus tree that stood tall and strong—a guardian to a valley under threat from industrial scale destruction. High up in its branches, a small platform was suspended by ropes that ran from the tree down to a freshly plowed logging road that cut it's way through the forest like a wound. The ropes were tied to structures built across the road, blocking the access of any logging machinery. Known as Camp Flozza, this blockade was the only thing standing between the lush rainforest and tall eucalyptus of the Upper Florentine Valley in Tasmania—and the bulldozers and chainsaws of those hell-bent on tearing it all down.

By the light of the moon (or the twinkle of stars), I would climb a long rope up and up and up into the branches of Old Frontie on most nights. I climbed through the shadows of twisting sassafras trees until I emerged from the lower canopy, and looked out to The Needles Mountain Range and Mount Mueller silhouetted in the darkness. Below, on the logging road, remained the soft murmur of the last of my friends on watch for the night, the soft glow of the campfire and the wisp of smoke rising up into the night sky.

Sometimes the nights would be dense with rain. Water would run down the inside of my sleeves, and pool around the bottom of my pants, while my painfully cold fingers gripped the rope. I would have a moment of jealousy towards those cozy under the tarp by the fire. But only a moment...because I knew that I had the best bed in the whole camp...maybe in the whole world! When I woke up in the morning, and peered out from the tarp that covered the small platform, I never failed to smile. A brilliant sunrise would be turning Old Frontie from silver to gold, lighting up each leaf as if glitter had been tossed out of the sky.

It was with Old Frontie, I first saw snow. My first winter at Camp Flozza, on a very cold night, I climbed the rope with numb fingers. I sat out in the snow for hours that night, perched on a branch, watching it gather on the tarp, the platform, the branches, my pants, jumper, shoes, and rope. Finally I went to sleep. And woke in the morning to a wonderland of white beneath me. Looking down over the forest, I saw the sassafras, myrtle, and celery-top pines bending under the weight of the white snow, clinging in clumps to their tiny leaves, while tree ferns made amazing patterns.

I came to know the patterns of Old Frontie. The changes over the seasons, the regular birds that visited...and I fell in love with that tree. I was full of spirit, rebellion, and hope. Old Frontie and I—we were a team guarding the forest, and there was no way we were going to let those loggers come and take this valley. As I lay nestled against the trunk of the tree, I would think of all the places I loved in the beautiful valley, with its groves of moss-draped sassafras and eucalyptus.

Old Frontie and I did the best we could, and we saved much of the forest. Forestry Tasmania had planned fifteen logging coupes within a three year period in the Upper Florentine. Portions were tragically logged. The rest still stand to this day, because of Camp Flozza. We fought a hard battle, as a community standing it's ground to save a pristine ecosystem—versus the weight of the forest industry propped up by plenty of money, political maneuvering, and policing. We won a lot of ground, but my heart will always ache for the friend I lost on the front lines.

I will never forget the day that Old Frontie was felled. We all were doing the best we could to halt the machines, but with the state's resources turning the police force into private security for the logging industry, things were getting tough. It was a crisp morning and we were all sitting by the side of Gordon River Road, tired and weary from trying and failing to halt the police invasion of our camp. When I saw the blue-uniformed man walking towards us, I knew why... I don't know how, but I had a sudden bad feeling... I knew what they were about to do. It was not that Old Frontie was even earmarked for logging, being situated outside the boundaries of the logging coupe. However, there is a tradition here in Tasmania—of taking down favorite trees for vengeance.

An impenetrable line of police stood guard while the chainsaw started up. And after all those years of defending the tree, I stood there. I just stood there and watched. Even though I wanted to run, screaming and throwing myself wildly at the police, I knew I'd be arrested in seconds and the execution would continue unhindered. So I stood there, silent as the sound of the chainsaw roared through the valley. I stood there, silent as the sound of cracking wood echoed into the distance. I stood there, silent as the ground shook from a fallen giant. And then I sat down, silent as Old Frontie lay sprawled across the forest floor, and cried.

They cut down Old Frontie to break us. But hundreds and thousands of trees awaited the same fate. In the memory of my brave friend, I would fight on...my wounded heart held a battle scar to remind me of why I could not let them win.

I tell this story because this is to be a story about two trees: the one that holds me in it's arms right now, as well as the one that I still hold dear in my heart. This is a tale about learning to love again. Because I cannot deny that when something changed in me that day that Old Frontie fell, I believed that to keep on doing what I needed to protect these forests, I needed to keep my heart safe. I had to build an impenetrable armor. And so on December 14, 2011, I climbed 60 meters up into a eucalyptus tree with this armor fixed tight around my heart…or so I thought. I would stay until the forest was saved, but the journey took me by surprise.

It was four months before my ascent that the Australian and Tasmanian governments had promised to place an immediate conservation agreement over 430,000 hectares of forest in Tasmania. This tree was among the many that would be saved. Yet, the plan was never properly implemented. And all around the state, precious ancient forests were falling to chainsaws. I wanted to do something to expose the truth. When I climbed this tree, and launched "Observer Tree," the idea was that I would film the logging as it occurred, and upload it for the world to see. I brought up to the platform everything I would need to survive for an unlimited amount of time: food, water, electrical equipment complete with solar panel, a swag to sleep in, and of course, a tough and guarded heart. I was prepared to sit there, and bear witness to any destruction that occurred around me.

After two days, I heard a voice calling from below. I looked down to see a high-vis clad man peering up. I braced myself for potential aggression, but instead he simply said that he was saying good-bye—the loggers were packing up and leaving! I was amazed that it had happened so quickly, perhaps scared away by the media spotlight that was now shining on this patch of forest.

I stayed in the tree. For over a year, I have looked out across the trees that surround me, knowing that they would have been a wasteland of burnt stumps by now, if I had not. This tree and all those around me would become toilet paper, coffee tables, and floorboards across the globe. Sadly, the thought hangs over my mind like a dark shadow... any day they could return, any day I could wake up to the sound of chainsaws once again.

My commitment to stay until protection was guaranteed remained unwavering. And so I stayed...and stayed. The weeks turned into months, a year came and went. It's been over sixty weeks now, but it was only after two that I noticed the small cracks in my armor. Without meaning to, I had let this forest soak into my heart. I had begun to notice the patterns of this tree and the landscape around me. I had begun to feel the tree's constant presence beside me, holding me up. And so a friendship grew. Slowly and intimately.

When I first made my new home here in the branches of "Tree," I did not want to arrogantly assume that we would have a connection. I wasn't necessarily welcome here. So I just waited and observed. I observed the tree in its forest, with its insects, birds, and animals. By doing so, I came to know the patterns and routines of this tree. And I began falling in love. I came to love every crease in the bark, every little hollow where spiders retreat and where Tasmanian skinks dart out, the hanging strips of bark that peel away day by day, the flowers that have sprouted, blossomed, and floated away.

I have watched the seasons come and go for two years now. Summers slowly turned into winters, bringing its snow. With "Tree" my only constant companion and friend, the connection deepened as I became a part of the landscape. I have seen new growth covering the tree in bright green and orange foliage, young shoots breaking through thick layers of bark as a tiny leaf emerges. I watch spiders weave, honey eaters search through bark for food, eagles circle, and the daily routines of animals and insects making their rounds.

My eyes trace the lines of bark that wrap around the tree's trunk. The patterns and shades I know so well. A voluntary smile breaks across my face. Like the smile between friends—the kind of friend that you know as well as you know yourself. I watch the raindrops gather in little lines on the underside of my tree's branches. The leaves become heavy and start to droop with the weight of water droplets that slide gracefully down the leaf's spine, hesitating for a moment at the very tip, before letting go. I reach my hand out to the branch—the one that makes a window for my view of this forest. I touch the creases and wrinkles that gather underneath. They are like the soft wrinkled folds of my Nana's skin, but without the softness of flesh. The wood is hard beneath my hand.

We bear heat, snow, and storms together. I have watched branches dance in the wind. And when the wind is high, the tree sways, and so do I. Wildly, the whole forest turns into a roaring ocean of waves as the trees are swirled this way and that. My platform is like a boat in a storm as I grip the ropes to keep my balance. I marvel at the strength of "Tree" to withstand such torrents, bending and flexing with the force of the wind. I learn a lot about strength and resilience from this tree.

More so, I have learned much about love and connection. This time, I fell in love with a forest, bare of illusion. I know that if they come to tear this place apart, that I can do nothing against their chainsaws, money, and arrogance borne of an incomprehensible lack of connection to that which they destroy. Perhaps my most profound lesson...is how powerfully loving the forest can be. It is a power that can save this tree and hundreds of thousands of others.

The risk of opening my heart to this magnificent forest around me, and this tree, has been worth it. It is through my connection with "Tree" that thousands of others have found a connection too. From this tiny platform perched high up in the middle of a remote Tasmanian forest, my tree and I have 'virtually' traveled the world, sharing our story. With solar power and internet access, I have updated a regular blog about my life in the treetops. I have Skyped with conferences, festivals, and schools across the globe. Thousands have come along on this journey with me, and know my tree, the intricacies of its patterns, its birds and insects, shrouding mists, sunrises that turn it's green leaves to gold. People who will never set foot in this forest...have had the chance to see it through my experience. The power of this shared experience has engaged people who have come to love this tree with a connection that inspires them to take a stand. I know that I, alone, may not be able to keep the chainsaws at bay—but together I believe we can.

As I look out across this forest I feel a sense of hope. I know that this tree will not fall with the sound of a chainsaw and my silent tears. If they ever come to cut down this tree, it will resonate across the globe. Others will support our trees and help. Because chainsaws are carving their way through trees across this island, for all of those precious ancient ecosystems in Tasmania, which have now been verified by scientists as national and World Heritage value, I will remain on my tree perch. For as long as it takes.

I imagine the day when I finally touch my feet on the earth below. I hope that I do so in celebration, with the declaration of this forest as World Heritage, safely protected for future generations. Then one day, when the time comes, this tree will fall on its own accord, yet still continue to bring life to this ecosystem as it becomes home to new creatures, gives nutrients to the forest floor, and continues the cycle of life in these ecosystems that have been evolving here for millennia. I will forever hold a special place in my heart for this tree, and the love I have found amongst the upper canopy of this gentle giant.

FOLLOW-UP NOTE: On March 7, 2013, Miranda reluctantly descended from "Observer Tree" to the ground, because of a wildfire threat nearby. Her incredible 449 days in the tree ended, but Miranda's campaign to save native forests goes on—with global support! In June 2013, the World Heritage Committee made a unanimous decision to give World Heritage status to Tasmanian forests, and again in 2014, to maintain this status, after the Australian government attempted to have portions of forest removed from the list.

"Observer Tree" will live on.

Snow covered trees,
the sound of an oar
striking still waters.

      *Calen Rayne

Stuck in waters
of a river gorge…
a leaf of some unknown tree.

      *Calen Rayne

Layers

by Shiila Safer

be with yourself long enough to go through the layers
releasing busyness and activity of the mind
opening to images, sensations, feelings,
glimpses of a deeper reality
underneath the layers
sink into it
surrender to it
let stillness envelope you
blessed peace and presence
subtlety of sounds
heightened awareness
timelessness
spaciousness
expansiveness

all yours in a moment
the gifts of spending time with yourself
with the Earth, the Trees,
the touch of the air on your skin
the flutter of wings nearby
anchor this feeling in your body
and carry it with you into your day
at the core of your being—Stillness

Ancestral Trees

by Wynn Renee Freeland
illustrated by Cheryl Elms

I used to sit by a pond between two beautiful willow trees when I lived in Sugar Land, Texas. It was a time of meditation for me—a beautiful respite when I was working as a therapist, and needed to clear my mind. I would walk for about forty-five minutes, and end my walk by sitting on a bench between the trees. One willow sensuously draped her lush green head of willow leaves into the pond. It always seemed like she was allowing herself to enjoy the glory of the sparkling pond water; her alluring tree branch hair gently floated, as if rocking a newborn babe. She spoke of a relaxing feminine strength, which reminded me of a very ancient story hidden within me. The other tree on my left, also a willow, stood tall with a strong back. He was a reminder of flexible strength, wisdom, and might through his straight back. I sat between the trees for months—almost every day.

One day a song came to me from the trees! I had been in the Earthtribe for a few years, and had heard others sing "Vision Songs," amazed that it was Nature speaking to them through music. As a born musician, I had never experienced a song from Nature. I started playing the piano when I was eight years old, and became a singer at the same age. I continued musical training, studying as a classical vocalist for thirty years, before switching to jazz in my late thirties. I intermittently sang professionally as an avocation, until into my forties.

Yet on this day in Sugar Land, as I gazed upon the sunny dancing diamonds on the pond water, I heard the trees whispering a song to me. Literally whispering in the same way that we talk to one another in our day-to-day conversations—no, not like that—a unique whisper to the depths—one might call it my essence, my soul—it doesn't matter. It felt similar to a soft feather caressing the part of me existing throughout eternity. As I write, I have visions of a baby discovering her feet and tenderly playing with them. I see a white swan progressively flying just above the water, skimming the water, landing in the water—majestic elegance. So, I can't really say the trees whispered in the way we usually think of as whispering.

I don't recall if the words or the music came to me first. I believe the song merely evolved. The piano arrangement for "Ancestral Trees" continued to emerge (or pollinate) after I quit attending the Earthtribe. This arrangement of "Ancestral Trees" touches the center of Mother Earth with strong roots. She sings a love song, and expresses her deep wounding. Just when you think she has been so wounded she will not recover, she carries you to the stars.

O' trees of beauty,
O' trees of might,
Within your wisdom,
I find Ancestral (Angelic) Light.
I've searched the world over,
And I come back to you.
O' trees of beauty
I Love you, I do.

Gifts from the Maple Tree

by Karen Smith

When you live with a maple tree for a whole year,
    you eventually stop fussing,

with any grace at all, about Spring's big messes

She makes with those tiny red beads and strings
    floating to the ground

each day from the maple tree's branches.

You simply understand that they too,
    these messy beads and strings,

are vital to the maple tree.

May we be gifted with the vision
    to see all of our own messy

beads and strings in the Spring.

    May we be gifted with the vision
        to see all the beautifully messy beads

and strings of the people in our lives.

    Our gift is to honor each other as we do the maple tree.

Tree School

by R.Maya Briel

illustrated by Gyorge Ann Wecker Yawn

So many of us sought comfort in forests and with trees, as children. The stories are boundless. I, myself, have had many experiences. My father made his living from the forests of Montana, so trees supported my family. I always think that I am somehow balancing those gifts by listening and learning from trees.

From the very beginning, trees were my friends. Even before I was a teen, I found comfort in their branches or at the base of their strong trunks. When I was five, my mother told me she could not coax me down from the tippy top of a huge Douglas fir that grew beside our country home. She was terrified that I would fall—I had climbed as high as my weight would allow, in a windstorm, so that the tree could rock me to and fro without breaking. I wasn't afraid; I loved the nurturing presence and touch. When I needed peace, there was a tranquil mossy spot at the base of a huge mother tree that grew beside our little creek. I still go to that place in my memories when I need peace and calming.

Pine trees were also an essential part of Christmas for my family. Not just because we traditionally went out to the forest to harvest our family Christmas tree, but also because our Christmas money came from pine boughs. I was the agile "little monkey" that could climb trees the best. I would scurry up to the level I needed to begin cutting pine branches for Christmas wreaths. One must always cut from the top down, so that there is a place to sit while sawing. Afterward, we would load up the branches, and take them into town. From there, they would be shipped all over the United States as Christmas wreaths, so that people without trees could have the aroma of pine for Christmas.

I don't remember exactly when my relationship with trees got more specific. Perhaps it was in my late twenties, when I sat with Grandmother Cottonwood. She was a good first teacher. I was intrigued, noticing that her roots spread out widely searching for water, while she towered up and over all the other trees. That was different from my pine and fir friends, whose presence was tightly rooted and protective. Her energy moved up, searching for the sun, and at the same time, back down in search of water and earth to sustain her. And so, I modeled myself after the cottonwood. A part of me is always reaching up, seeking the light of who I am, while staying rooted deep in the loamy earth and water that feeds my human growth. I guess we need both.

As I look back over my life with trees, I feel how blessed I have been. I have traveled the world observing and learning from trees. From the redwoods in California, whose presence has borne witness to more years and change than any of us can imagine—to the Joshua trees in Nevada, which grow so slowly that one would not guess their gnarled barren bodies are among the oldest on the planet—to the root balls of the ancient olive trees in Israel that can go dormant for hundreds of years—to the Dawn redwoods who lost their lives to the Yangtze dam project—to the endangered Huan pine in Tasmania which provided the best ships and masts for sailing ships to explore our seas—to the Siberian pines which are fed as much from the sky energy as from their roots. Yes, I can go on…they are so varied and unique. Trees bridge the etheric sky energy with the soil from Mother Earth. They are vast producers of oxygen, which we all need to breathe. They provide life for so many species on our planet. They have all been my healing and energetic teachers. I am happy that my conscious awareness included opening my eyes, ears, and heart to trees. So blessed, to be still breathing and listening and learning.

backyard bliss

by rashida alisha hagakore

making a small yard a mini-paradise of delight!
grateful for what you got
    + imagination
        + need for nature connection
            = urban goddess maneuvers.

trees are antennas:
|| grounded + reaching out ||
~ roots down | branches up ~

they teach by being and i love being with them

Time Is Stilled in These Ancient Groves

by Osprey Orielle Lake
illustrated by Cheryl Elms

Along the northern California coast, there are gigantic denizens that command our attention, ancient ones who reach back far in time, some more than several thousand years. When you look up, you cannot see the top of these titans; that is how tall and expansive the coastal redwoods are.

On an excursion to the Lost Coast, I ventured to one of the few old-growth redwood forests still standing just north of Garberville, the "Avenue of the Giants," to meet Mary Anne Kenney, an elderly woman and a dear friend.

Thin rays of light streamed through the feathered needles of the forest. The palatial trees filled the entire sky, allowing only small shafts of sunlight through the treetops like ribbons of molten glass. The shimmering sunrays reached downward to the cool bed of the forest floor, glancing off the top of my head as a warm greeting.

What is illuminated in a redwood forest is only what the upper branches reveal at any given time of day. Beyond this, there is only a blue glow within the ancient groves, which seems to come directly from the trees themselves, as well as a deep quiet that arrests all outer and inner chatter. I come here to listen to the venerable wisdom of the forest, from trees who are much older than the human species, and who are, indeed, our ancestors. These trees are my relatives and I am honored to walk amongst them and allow myself to behold their majesty.

One redwood must have felt the footsteps of a familiar friend who had been to the forest many times before. I watched as Mary Anne placed her hands in the folds of the deep furrows of the tree trunk. The stately woman leaned her body forward, looking up the column, eyes searching for the hidden firmament above. I marveled at how my friend's finely wrinkled face and hands blended with the crevices and woven strands of the fibrous bark. For a moment, human and tree became one. Time is stilled in these old groves, and the mind lifts and tunes itself to the hum of the ages.

Mary Ann and I have walked here many times before. I come here to council with the trees as much as with my long-time friend. She and I know our conversations are heightened and transformed when we speak within the unwavering power and mystery of these woodlands.

The coastal redwoods are the tallest trees on Earth and have survived here for more than seventy-five million years. Individuals can grow up to three hundred and sixty feet tall and can live longer than two thousand years. The oldest recorded tree was a coastal redwood named "Eon" in Humboldt County, which fell in 1977, and was estimated to be a startling 6,200 years of age.

While these very old trees have much to teach us about survival and endurance, they now exist only as a minuscule living museum in small corridors along the north coast, after more than a century of timber cutting. The journey to the California redwoods is bittersweet: the trees are still there, which is cause for celebration; yet, the old-growth forests have been mostly exterminated.

The ribbon of coastal redwoods in California typically extends about twenty miles inland, but in Mendocino County it reaches about forty miles east because of rivers and valleys that allow the fog (the key maritime climatic requirement for these trees) to drift further. These remarkable titans are so tall that ground water cannot make its way past the capillary-action limit of three hundred feet to the upper branches, so the top is watered through the upper flat needles by osmosis with the fog. In addition, during the long rainless summers in this region, these top feathery leaves, perfectly designed to capture water droplets from the misty coastal air, provide water to the roots as it drips to the ground. Redwoods can also generate their own fog using huge amounts of transpiring moisture condensed at night above the cool valley groves.

Redwoods are also known for their special bark. This fibrous red bark is very thick and contains no resin, making the trees remarkably fire resistant and resilient. It is also a surprise to learn that these tallest of trees do not have deep-anchored roots, but rather shallow ones, reaching down only some six or eight feet. The secret to their upright strength is in the intertwining and actual joining of their massive roots, which radiate out horizontally several hundred feet. These interconnected roots stabilize the trees in flood conditions and high winds, and they can also share water through this extensive root system. In addition to the conjoined roots, during big winter storms the arms of the trees literally swim in the wind, as if treading water, to keep the trees upright.

Each time I pick up a redwood seed cone from the forest floor I am startled at its size, which is about the same as a grape's, and the seed itself, which is roughly the size of a rice grain. How can such a tiny seed grow into the tallest tree in the world? I wonder, is it possible that the smallest seeds we carry in the quiet of our hopeful hearts can grow into the very greatest and most noble things?

These trees are also unique because, besides the germination of seeds, they can also reproduce by sprouting from a root burl, creating a ring of smaller trees. Sometimes you can see several generations of trees growing around one central hollow where the parent tree once existed. It's a family circle of sorts, and it is thought that some redwoods actually contain the identical genetic codes of trees millions of years old—that is, a redwood of today can be birthed from a prehistoric one.

Sadly, only about four percent of the redwoods that grew along the Pacific coast before logging still exist, which has caused ongoing battles up and down the region, as people have put their very lives on the line to save the last of these grand "keepers of time." There are legendary women from this area, who have risked life and limb because of their dedication to these trees—notably Judi Bari and Julia Butterfly Hill—and I remember them each time I visit the forest. Starting at the age of seventeen, I worked on a campaign to protect the redwoods along the Big River Watershed, which skirts the southern end of the town of Mendocino. During that time, the many biologists and environmentalists who fought for the trees were my champions (and they still are). I have learned that these redwood battles are always complex, but no matter what opinion or inclination a person might have toward the future of these forests, one thing is certain: no one with any sensitivity can be in the presence of these ancients without experiencing enormous inspiration, and a tremendous feeling of awe. More than once I have seen people with tears in their eyes along these backwoods trails.

In 1861, Hans Christian Andersen wrote of the future and promise of poetry in his work, *The New Century's Goddess*. This literary piece, in which Andersen elaborates on his hope for new freedom of thought, posits a few places as the possible origin of this New Goddess of poesy, and one of them is the stately redwood forest of California.

From Andersen:

"The New Century's Goddess—whom our great-grand-children or perhaps a still later generation will know, but we shall not—when and how does she reveal herself?
What does she look like?
What is the theme of her song?
Whose heartstrings will she touch?
To what heights will she lift her century?
Each century, each thousand years, one might even say, has its chief expression in its poetry. Born in the passing era, it comes forth and reigns in the new, succeeding era.
When begins the New Age of Poesy?
When will the Goddess be known?
When will she be heard?

Will she come from the newfound land of Columbus,
the land of freedom, where the native is hunted and the
African is a beast of burden, the land from where we
heard The Song of Hiawatha?
Or from the antipodes, that golden nugget in the south-
ern sea, the land of opposites, where our nighttime is
their daytime, and where the black swans sing in mossy
forests?
Or maybe from the land where Memnon's pillar rings
but we never understood the Song of the Sphinx in the
desert from the isle of the coal pit, where, since the age
of the great Elizabeth, Shakespeare has reigned?
Or from Tycho Brahe's home, where he wasn't wanted;
or from California's fairyland, where the redwood holds
high its crown as king of the earth's forests? Greetings,
you Goddess of the New Century!"

Walking in these forests, "California's fairyland," I ponder
Andersen's words and wonder how we are doing in regard to his
salutation sent down to us through time and heard beyond "the
clatter of engines, the screams of locomotives, the thunder of
quarry blasts" of his day. From my place in the coastal redwoods,
I am attempting to greet this New Century's Goddess by holding
a lantern up for her appreciation and emancipation. The promise
of her freedom is rooted in America's soil, the Indigenous people
of this land, and in the hearts of all people learning to be at home
here from their various places of origin.

Love's Web

By Patricia Varney

Daycare: As a child I lived in the Adirondacks of northern New York State. I did not wish to neglect my dolls while I engaged in "tomboy" pursuits, such as tadpole-watching, softball, or swimmin' in the Hudson River. So, on weekend mornings, I'd climb the pine trees in my backyard, place one of my "babies" securely in the arms of each tree, climb back down, and repeat this task until all were secure. I knew the wind would help rock them until I came back. At the end of my busy day, I'd repeat this process in reverse, asking each doll how her day had been, knowing they'd had the best of care.

Hideaway: One of the pines in my backyard had a huge branch that lowered from the trunk to the ground, creating a small cave of greenery. Whether I was lonely or wished to avoid others, that pine held me in sweet privacy from toddler to teens.

Faeries: Youthful summer vacations were spent helping on the "tabacca farm" of my maternal grandmother, in Virginia. Miles from others my age, I often grew tired of the "old folks." I'd escape to the mossy trunks of the trees, in a fairyland grove near the farmhouse. There, I'd fashion miniature furniture of moss, chattering with the faeries I could never quite see. I felt their presence, and their delight in my gifts. Such wondrous company for a young girl.

Hospice: My Aunt and Mother were soon to die. It was an inescapable fact. I set off on a Vision Quest, in Texas. All I could do that first day was huddle close to Mother Earth, and sob. Spent, I finally noticed my surroundings. I'd chosen a site with ten trees within my "prayer ties protection." Eight were sisters murmuring comfort, as I lay at their feet in their snug circle of embrace. Each one represented a direction. Emptied of hoarded grief, I was free to experience the peace that was present in Love's Web.

Cedar Communing: In the graveyard near my present home, a huge Grandmother Cedar grows in such a way that an adult can squirm through the opening and stand within its trunk. When I do so, I am about a foot off the ground—almost completely surrounded by the tree trunk. I do not know what injury could have caused this, nor how the tree continued to grow. Still, I feel more comfort from relatives who have passed, when I am within this tree, than when I am standing by their graves.

Miracle in the Jungle

by Joy Phoenix

illustrated by Kerri Hummingbird Lawnsby

I was raised in New Zealand minutes from where 'Rivendell' was filmed in the movie *Lord of the Rings*. Like my Elvin neighbors I tend to get along better with trees than with most people.

As a shaman I have learned that all great trees have Nature Spirit Guardians that grow with them in a perfect symbiotic relationship. Together the tree and its Guardian look after the surrounding area, acting as home and sanctuary for many creatures, and protecting the earth under, and often far beyond, the tree's root system.

Tree Guardians don't usually show themselves, they have learned the hard way that it's not a good idea. Mankind doesn't have a good track record with nature.

To see them, one must look more with one's heart than with the eyes. And you must be willing to let them see your heart to gauge the purity of your intent.

You can talk, and more importantly listen, to Nature Spirits with a quiet mind and an open heart. Their wisdom is grounded and patient. They know how to withstand drought and flood, winter and summer, and how to keep growing toward the sun regardless of what else is happening. When I lay my troubles at the base of my favorite tree she gently asks "How will this matter in a hundred years?"

I've had wonderful things happen when I improve the environment around Guardian trees. Picking up rubbish is the fastest, easiest, most immediately impactful way to give thanks and give back. This has resulted in surprising miracles.

My favourite example is a story of instant karma and tree hospitality that takes place in a jungle near Puerto Vallarta, Mexico.

I had gone with friends for a healing mud massage day, and left them frolicking in the pools and waterfalls by our camp. I scheduled myself last in line for massage so I would have three hours to explore this remote piece of paradise.

We were far from anyone and anything, so I took off upstream for a deeper connection with nature.

Soon I was out of sight and away from any sign of civilization. I left my clothes on a friendly tree and waded for a mile or so through knee deep water until I reached a place of ancient and beautiful magic, then I opened my heart and stood soul exposed before the spirits of that place.

"I Am JOY! I come in love, and ask permission to enter this space. How may I serve?"

I waited until I received a returning welcome, which came as a warm inviting wave of energy from the guardian of a beautiful tree about 100 yards upstream. She was young with the stately manner of a princess, and she was curious about me.

I approached with reverence and excitement "Greetings sister, can we play?" I gently sent my energy out to brush against hers, and felt a responding tingle of acceptance and invitation.

I had a heightened awareness of the nature spirits around me; they were observing, not coming out to play but not hiding either.

The river was soft and cool around my legs and as I got closer to the tree I had to stop and pay homage, the beauty of the place was overwhelming. I knelt on a rock exactly the size of my crouching body, it was covered in the softest of underwater ferns and felt exactly like a really thick feather boa.

I knelt there absorbing everything with wonder, so grateful, and a little concerned. I'm a pale redhead, and the sun was very hot on my naked body, I could feel my skin beginning to burn and knew I'd be in a bad way after three hours.

"Don't worry" I was assured, *"all that you need is provided."*

"OK, well, I guess the mud will help the sunburn, and I'll stay in the shade as much as possible. I give thanks and release my concern, I will not allow this to spoil my adventure."

I looked up from my position on the rock in the middle of the river toward my Tree Guardian friend. She stood beyond a row of tiny waterfalls, and in front of a striking rock formation.

To the left of me was a tiny curved 'beach' of grainy sand about 10 feet across, to my right a grove of trees clustered like maiden aunts making sure nothing was amiss.

My eye was drawn to a piece of rubbish caught on the top of one of the waterfalls. That would never do. I went over to retrieve it.

Right next to it, unseen until I picked up the trash, was a full tube of 30+ sunscreen, waterproof to 80 minutes.

Now that's my kind of miracle! Completely practical, totally unexpected, instant karma, physical proof that it really is TRUE, all that I need really *is* magnetized toward me. There couldn't be better proof than a tube of sunscreen in the middle of the jungle just when I needed it!

I would never have seen the sun block if I hadn't removed the rubbish.

Such an efficient little test of whether or not I meant "How may I serve?"

The day just got better and better after that.

My gracious Tree hostess laid on everything my heart could desire. Jacuzzi waterfalls to massage me, a beautiful bed of soft sand, sheltered on three sides and from above by an elaborate rock formation. There were butterflies the size of bread and butter plates, and lizards and iguanas to laze with me as I floated in tranquil pools watching the play of light and shadow in the glow of nature unbound.

I stood next to my beautiful tree friend, so delighted to have shared this time and space with her, to experience all of this. Next thing the little branch I was holding came off in my hand!

I was appalled! Oh NO, she has shown me nothing but courtesy and I repay it by breaking a limb?

She quickly assured me that it was a gift, and I looked again. The limb was a couple of feet long, very light weight with softly mottled green and brown bark, and a wild orchid air plant growing on the end of it. Nice!

I bade her a grateful farewell. It was time to head back for my massage.

As the clay drew toxins out of my body I ruminated on how much healing I'd already received from my tree friend that day. And how wonderful it is that we don't have to be in a far-flung tropical paradise to receive healing from a tree. They are willing to offer healing to anyone who seeks it, no matter who or where.

Go to a tree you feel drawn to and position yourself comfortably against it. Breathe deeply allowing yourself to relax more and more into the tree with every breath. Imagine you are growing roots to entwine with the roots of the tree.

Imagine opening the top of your head to inhale light, and the rich oxygen the tree has been producing. Draw it down through your crown, down through your trunk, down through your limbs, down through your roots and into the earth.

Let it wash away anything you want to clear from your body, mind or spirit. Let everything that no longer serves you drain out of your body, through your roots. Offer it to the tree as a gift of compost.

When you feel clear, breathe healing and nourishment up from the tree, up through your roots, up through your limbs, up through your trunk, up through your crown and into the sky. Keep 'Tree Breathing' until you feel complete.

When it's time, gently bring your roots back into your body. Take three deep breaths. Feel how you feel now, and offer love and gratitude to the tree to complete the cycle. ☺

Come Home

by Larry Winters

I am lost
at dusk I go
to where the river meets the trees
I speak to the sky reflected at my feet
I raise my arms
free my soul to the breeze
my eyes catch starlight in the tree branches
on the rivers face
sky and river the same
heat-lightning in the clouds
is my heartbeat in the night sky
in my way I reach
the trees whisper
come home.

Li'l Boab

by Ashe Godfrey

illustrated by Cheryl Elms

It was the first time I had ever travelled from my home in Perth, Western Australia to Sydney in New South Wales. I had recently lost a very close friend to cancer, and he had come to me in spirit form. It was a very profound experience, because it was my "first." So after that, I kept myself open to seeing him again wherever I went, and expected him to reappear on this, my "first" real adventure.

It was only a three-day holiday, so it was all quite a rush to see the sights, and take in the energy and vibrations of the biggest city in Australia. One of the places I really wanted to visit was the Botanical Gardens. We did this on a bright and sunny day, with a nice breeze coming from the Sydney Harbour where the Gardens nestled. My partner and I enjoyed the quiet surrounds after leaving the craziness of life, and our five kids, back in Perth. It was beautiful and relaxing, and we were feeling so happy to be there.

Strolling the Gardens, we saw some unusual and fascinating trees. As we moved along, I happened to glance back—and there he stood with his li'l fat belly: A BOAB TREE! I was so surprised to see him there—and we had nearly walked straight past him! He was tucked away in a corner all by himself, surrounded by lawn. Straight away, I was drawn to him, and felt the strongest urge to give him a big huge hug. This was yet another "first" time experience for me. I was communicating with a tree, and it was quite surreal and very powerful.

I had a really strong sense of his loneliness and that he missed his home. He really didn't understand what he was doing there (these trees are native to northern Australia, and places like Madagascar and Brazil). It brought me back to a childhood memory, when my family and I drove all along the top of Australia to Cairns. We had stopped at Derby, and saw the Boab Jail tree, located where indigenous Australians had been kept at a rest-stop prison.

Thankfully, my partner is very accepting of my quirky nature—especially after the last few months of communicating with the spirit world—and took some pleasing photos of me with my new tree friend. I gave Li'l Boab the biggest hug, and promised I would try to help his loneliness.

I realised that I had not quite absorbed the gravity of this situation, until that night when I got back to my hotel and thought about it. I was quite upset that I did not get a chance to just sit with him and see what else he wanted to say. More so, I wanted to learn more! We had to leave early the next morning, so it was impossible to let him know that I had heard him loud and clear, even if it had taken me a little while to process this rare event. I got it. All he wanted was to be back where he belonged, where the weather was hot and the dirt was red. A place where I had been born and understood and loved—the raw beautiful country where we were both from—but I couldn't do that for him. So, I had to figure out what I could do!

I felt great sadness flying back to Perth and not being able to see him again. Once home, looking at photos, I was just wracked with guilt that this Li'l Boab had told me how he felt and I was now all the way on the other side of Australia. I could even see his face with his branches out-stretched ready for a cuddle! How could I help him?

I called up my very special friend, Fiona, with whom I can talk about all manner of things. (Most people think you'd be a bit crackers when you mention talking to trees.) She came up with the idea of making a "HUG ME" sign to place right in front of him. I got quite excited about that idea. Because he sees so many tourists, Li'l Boab would be getting hundreds of hugs a day. BRILLIANT!

So that night I decided to write an email to the Sydney Botanical Gardens, hoping they could construct a "HUG ME" sign just for Li'l Boab. I was quite hopeful they would take me seriously. I mean, how hard is it to make a "HUG ME" sign, and put it up? It could be a tourist attraction!

Unfortunately, the response was quite defensive, explaining that they take good care of their trees—which of course they do on a physical level. I really wish I had worded my letter in such a way that they didn't feel I was accusing them of neglect—which was far from my mind. I was just excited that I had the privilege of being given a message from a tree. I don't think that the particular responder realized that trees have feelings, too—putting out generational vibrations.

I really feel Li'l Boab was able to communicate with me, because I had left myself open for my dear departed friend to be able to reach me from beyond this world. I'm on a mission to get back to Li'l Boab as soon as I can, and spend more time with him. I hope that everyone who reads this book will be sure to pay my tree friend a visit, if they ever get a chance to visit Sydney. He is located near the Wishing Tree and the Maiden Pavilion—off the pathway—so keep your eyes peeled!!

Pulsating like the stars,
the wiser trees observe without commenting:
humans will pass or, guided,
united to the world with us, they will have the stars…

Oberto Airaudi, "Falco"

The Betrothal Tree
at Emily Ann Theatre, Wimberley, Texas

by Dorey Schmidt

Here—with our hands
joined in this living tree,
standing on this hill
beneath God's sky—
I pledge myself to you
and you to me
with love that will not die—
everlasting as the stone
on which we stand
and ancient as this oak.

With arms entwined
our lips so softly touch,
and by this act we vow
our love is blessed,
both now and till the end
of measured time.

Lonely Child Finds Consolation with a Tree

written and illustrated by Reginah Brown Dove

I believe my first "real" relationship was with a tree. I loved her, and I knew she loved me. She supported my thoughts at a time in my life when I needed her desperately. I'll tell you the story...

I lived at a residential school during my youth, between 1948 and 1951. There was great pain in my heart at being separated from my family, and put into a school. At six years old, I was not able to comprehend the reasons. The tree I speak of (most likely an oak) resided in the backyard of the late 1930s two-story schoolhouse called, "Academy For Little Folk," in Los Angeles, California. Our relationship was not complicated. She was my best friend. All that was required was my daily presence. I never thought to give her a name. She was just mine.

I really believe that she taught me how to listen, and take advice from sources I would later learn to trust. Today the smell of crayons brings me back to my little wooden desk, where I would look out the window, and "talk" to my tree. She was waiting there for me. Many times my tears had rolled off that wooden desk, and my young heart had ached. The one stable element, that kept me hopeful, was that tree.

After a period of great struggling I came to love that school, despite having to sit with my green peas until they were gone from my plate. I could see my tree through a big window from the place I sat every night at the dinner table. Like a loving grandmother, she encouraged me to eat my vegetables. It seems so funny to me today, over 64 years later, to realize that the staff of the school had no idea that I was following directions from a tree on the property. They probably thought it was their skillful manners that moved me!

There were so many wonderful activities available at this school. But I did not always think they were wonderful. Yet my tree had everything to do with my ability to turn a sad situation into one of joy. When I did not want to go on field trips, because I thought I'd miss a visit from my parents, she would frown at me. I'd go, and then return from the trips with a gleeful report to the tree. Once we visited Griffith Park, a huge facility of acres and acres of wilderness with horses, squirrels and other wonderful creatures. We walked and ran all day. My tree never said anything like "I told you so." She looked at me with, what I would call today, unconditional love.

Although, what I am about to say may seem sad, for me it was miraculous. I don't remember when it started, but I know it seemed to last forever. I began imagining that I was being shot. Yes, with bullets; shot out of my tree after climbing it. I would fall "dead" on the ground, and lay there a few seconds before being resurrected—and going at it all over again. It seemed like I had climbed to the top; but I am sure it was only a couple of feet. Then I would rub circles of dirt on my arms to show where the bullets and arrows had "hit" me. My wounds were visible all over me. My tree loved it. She kept encouraging me to climb up again and again, until I was worn out; the original eco-spirit therapist! I believe this is how I was able to express my pain, my deep emotional grief, my overwhelming feelings of abandonment by my family. My parents had their reasons to leave my brother and I at the residential school, but any rational reason meant nothing to me.

Some would say these are just the psychological fantasies of a lonely child. I like to think of it as a special connection that we all have to the intelligence of nature, if we pay attention. Who are we to judge and label the value of a fantasy? A friendless child finds consolation with a tree. That ought to be enough.

Woodpine

by Lillie Rowden

Standing
Alone on the bank
By the living stream,
Dark and silent are the woods,
Hung with tangled limbs and vine,
—A glimmer of life
In the darkened flood,
Impatient small creature,
Free, imprisoned in your world,
Seeking you know not what, as I?
You can not leave by choice,
But only in pain,
Caught in the stillness
Of your time and place,
Beauty captured
On death's chance, sharp scythe,
Fleeing away—
Never seen again.
Time calls me back on the needled path
To cross into the busy world—
Yet, my heart lingers in the solitary gloom,
Man's heaven hidden from view,
Deep within a quiet Presence speaks,
I'm here in the silence,
Be still—
Come home.

The Big Oak Tree

by Marlan Healing Juniper

illustrated by Hollyana Melear

When I was a teenager in high school it was the early 70s: a time of peace, love, rock-n-roll, and mind-expanding experiences.

I experimented with many new things, one of which was LSD—which I truly believe expands the mind. I did not take drugs to escape reality, but instead to open up my consciousness. I wanted to find out more about our universe. I wanted to know more about who I was. As a child, I guess I just never got satisfied of nobody being able to answer my big question of "WHY?"

The guys I ran around with in high school were probably what most people call normal. They never wondered "WHY?". They only wanted to get high, laugh loud, and have sex. On the other hand, I wanted to discover the life force of the universe and tap into it. I wanted love, more than sex.

One weekend, my buddies and I went camping. It was going to be a grand weekend of getting high. There were probably seven or eight guys hanging out around the campfire, getting loaded and acting stupid. Our campsite was in the forest, and the fire was at the center of a small clearing which had a circle of really large oak trees. The fire pit was centered so the flames would not hit the branches.

I could feel that I was going in a different direction than my friends. I was losing my connection to them, and what seemed to matter to them did not matter to me, or vice versa. So I left the comfort of the fire, and walked down a dirt road for about a mile. I found a meadow and looked up. I saw the universe. I saw it like I had never seen it before. It was alive and I was part of it. There came forward the shape of a woman in the stars, and as she sparkled, I thought this must be the black magic woman that Santana had sung about.

I started to walk back to the fire, and while I was on the road I saw a large mound of dirt. I stopped and watched it unfold and stand up as a man. He had no face. He was of the earth, and he stuck out his hand to shake mine. I did not feel threatened. I don't recall feeling scared, but I didn't know what to do, so I took off for the comfort of the fire. When I got back, I realized that nothing had changed with my friends, so I did not bother trying to tell them about my experience.

What I did notice were the oak trees. They were like a circle of friends; arms sticking out touching the brother next to him; leaves waving like hair in the wind. My focus of comfort was now on the trees, not the fire. I think that since the beginning of man's connection with fire, he has been comforted by it more then anything else. But the connection to the earth and trees is a much older connection.

I started kind of a trance dance with the trees—like I was laughing and running and playing with them. Of course, my friends laughed at me, but I didn't care. Finally, I was with life forms who liked me for me. So then I took off all my clothes and climbed up into a tree about 20 feet high, and sat on a branch—just to be closer to my new friend. Of course, my high school friends got a hoot out of that, but for once I didn't care what anyone thought.

Sitting there for hours, I became part of the tree. I watched as ants crawled across my legs doing what ants do. The tree seemed to understand me, and for all my flaws—loved me. I thanked the earthman, which I had seen earlier on the road, for trying to connect with me. I think maybe he told the trees to talk to me. I had such a comfortable feeling with my new friends, I did not want it to end. I thought about the origin of man, and what a long story it was. Sitting on a branch, while visualizing that an ancestor must have done this before, I thought, "We are all connected. We cannot be without the tree, rock, or earth—we are all one."

I came down in the wee hours of the morning, went into the woods, found a creek flowing, and followed it up to where it was making a waterfall.

As the sun came up, the water flowing over the small waterfall sparkled like diamonds. I was glad to have been in that moment.

Over the years, I have shared this story with only a few people. It is one of my deepest heartfelt stories. I have a special connection with trees. They are my brothers and sisters.

Many years later, on a mountain during my second Vision Quest, I laid under the arms of a juniper tree who gave me strength and protected me. She reminded me of my friends, the oaks. I received the nature name "Healing Juniper."

When I think of intimacy, I think of trees. When I need to be flexible, I think of the willow. When I can't see the beauty in something, I visualize the turning of leaves in trees.

Love to you All
Marley Healing Juniper

Trees in autumn,
a clear mountain lake.
One gull... then another...

        Calen Rayne

Scarlet maple leaves
among solitary peaks,
twilight in Autumn.

        Calen Rayne

The Holy Book of Trees

by Bruce P. Grether

This book
Is not a book—
It's a forest — THE Forest
The Forest Primeval —
With everyone's Ancestors deep
DEEP within our trillions of cells;
Golden shafts of sunlight
Reach through, yet only
With the canopy's permission.

A thousand possibilities awaken
While creatures stir, stretch, turn and look about —
While a thousand others
Curl, breathe deeper, and though alert
Move towards sleep...
Here is found and here abounds
That green that cannot be more green
The soil of precise and perfect richness —
All is present and balanced.

You do not open this book's pages with your fingers —
For it is also the Book of Life
That opens with every breath you take
With each beat of your heart.

Compassionate Embrace
A Story of Co-Counseling With Trees

by Laurel Emrys

illustrated by Cathy Dyer

My life's work has always, in one way or another, involved the learning and practice of self-healing. This journey began for me in the early 1970s due to the onset of surprisingly severe spinal and neck pain, which became chronic over the years. One of my first forays into the world of healing was through a discipline called "Re-evaluation Counseling" (RC). And, to this day, it remains one of my most basic self-healing resources.

Before I get to the wondrous part that trees have played in my use of RC, I would like to share a summary of the process itself. RC is a form of peer counseling that provides tools and support for people to resolve distressing (or simply outmoded) patterns of thought and behavior—and it does so, primarily, through the vehicle of emotional release.

The key to the practice of RC is to recover one's natural capacity for emotional release, which involves freeing up four main human expressions of feeling: laughing, crying, shaking and yawning. Acting, alternately, as both RC counselor and client, participants learn how to elicit the conscious act of such physical discharge of emotions to regain a sense of peace and joy, which in turn, leads to the re-evaluation of one's distress.

The act of emotional re-evaluation could just as easily be called transformation. It is a spectacular event in any life. Distinguished from simply "changing," re-evaluation literally disappears the distress of past events, thoughts, and feelings which have destroyed emotional and/or physical health.

Are healing journeys conceived of as being efforts to fix oneself, or as journeys in the simple acceptance of being human?

When allowing feelings to discharge, an issue that was painfully distressing loses its sting and becomes simply "the past" or "just information."

Creating a "balance of attention" opens the way to discharge distress caused by feeling completely immersed, or unusually detached, from painful emotions. When overwhelmed by these emotions, a person loses the feeling of safety; when too detached, he/she becomes numb to feelings altogether, or redirects attention onto something else entirely. Numbness and desensitization blocks one from moving forward, lodging the pain deep within.

Consequently, it's the "balance of attention"—just the right amount of attention on the distress, and likewise, on that which is not distressing—which opens the way for discharge to flow with ease. Distress is always a function from the past. We've all experienced those moments when our "balance of attention" was stable, because emotions were discharged appropriately at the right time—allowing them to move through the process and relinquish any holds. It actually feels wonderful to discharge, doesn't it?

In the traditional RC setting, this "balance of attention" is achieved by the presence of a loving, attentive co-counselor. I have found this process to be so beneficial to my overall well-being that I've been co-counseling and teaching RC for more than four decades. However, one day I discovered that there was at least one other good way to create a productive "balance of attention," and it did not involve another person at all. It was all about the trees!

Here's what happened. Instead of a supportive human counselor to listen and pay loving attention to me, as a counterbalance to the feelings I need to discharge, I discovered that nature, and notably trees, do a fabulous job in nearly the same way. Trees "listen" and project love, and by doing so, provide beautiful support and guidance. In short, they provide the perfect "balance of attention" to open the floodgates for discharging.

Flowers, plants, and trees were trusted friends in the days of my childhood, when I grew up surrounded by the rolling hills and wide open pastures of the New Jersey countryside. On one side of our property was a 30-acre corn field. On the other was a pear orchard replete with Holstein cows. Every day that I watered my garden and engaged in long involved talks, especially with the sunflowers, it just seemed natural and relaxing to commune while happily engaged in this activity together. I found them to be friendly, helpful and darned chatty.

These pleasant childhood memories returned one day, when I was grown and living in Austin, Texas—feeling some powerfully strong emotional distress weighing me down—and not a human counselor in sight. I went out walking in the neighborhood park so I could dislodge some of the intense stress I was feeling. My mother had just died and I was in desperate need of comforting. In other ways, too, it was proving to be a sad and difficult period in my life, because I had already lost most of my family to death—and relationships were now eroding into extreme dissension among the living, because of the lack of good will between heirs. Not surprisingly, I was often overwhelmed. But on that day the burdened and motherless child in me sprang free under the glorious sun of the Texas Hill Country sky, when I took to the park and found myself quite alone in its verdant, welcoming, tree-lined expanse. What a luxury that was! I ended up walking back and forth along the paths where dear old cedars and lively oak trees were passionately swaying in the early summer wind. They seemed to be beckoning and I eagerly responded.

That's when I discovered how trees were ultra-willing to be my trusty co-counselors. As I was walking and talking—just as I would with a human counselor—I began to feel their presence fill me. They were no longer simply trees in a park; they became energies of light-filled compassion that reached forth and touched the pain I was holding onto, with intelligence and focus which was amazingly obvious. The more I opened up and let their energies embrace me, the more freely my emotional discharge flowed, and the more love I received from the trees touching my heart and whispering to me as I walked among them. Some had low voices that resonated me from the inside out; other voices were barely audible, high ephemeral sounds, reverberating my whole system far beyond what was normally touchable by forms of Mother Nature.

Friendly oak trees were situated so close to the path where I was walking, that their shade provided a welcome shelter from the heat, both external and internal. For at least an hour I walked and talked, cried and shook, ranted and raved, and asked for help. Sometimes the trees would "tell" me to be still and simply absorb their grounding, nurturing essence. Sometimes they would instruct me on specific things to say or do. Always, they would soothe my overwrought mind and ask me to relax into their leafy goodness...and so I did.

Not only could I feel the trees ministering to me through listening, caring, and encouragement...I could feel their supportive raw power holding and enfolding me. The touch of their huge force fields unleashed floodgates of emotions, which felt so satisfying and good, so cleansing and healing. Afterwards, as branches swayed, the trees moved into "wisdom mode," showering me with terse, pithy words and phrases that imparted perfectly matched truths—activating me to do exactly what I needed to do next. What a gift: I would ask a question and (yes!) receive an answer.

After that experience I knew that it didn't matter where I walked among the trees. It could be anywhere—a secluded backyard, a nearby park, or in the depths of a still forest. Tuning-in to the loving presence of my beloved tree co-counselors always made it so easy and pleasurable to laugh, cry, sigh, shake and yawn.

Like all superlative counselors, trees listen closely, connecting into the message behind the words. They radiate acceptance and embody the peace of wellness. I hear their tree "voices" loving me high and low, murmuring "all is well, dear one." I feel their roots forming a foundational sense of safety and security within, as I feel what I long to, letting these feelings fly, knowing I am OK just as I am. Tree "arms" hold me close, and as my heart resonates, a remarkably enriched tuning takes place.

And I, in spacious openness, receive tree wisdom, surging from the ground up through me, as I walk and talk among them, reverberating with the consciousness of being healed by the vibrational clarity of truth: tree truth. And from this exchange grace abounds! Whatever was bothering me disappears or lightens, noticeably, blessedly. Transformation becomes activated, and is now real for me; hot-button issues melt into being "just information" once again.

In the glory of their leaves, branches, and bark, the gifts of my tree counselors are infinitely helpful. And practical: there really couldn't be a more perfectly accessible source of support. My trees and your trees love to be there for us and with us...of this I am sure.

Nine Inches Of Rain

by Mariénne Kreitlow

Nine inches of rain fell in a week.
I weed and weed, a woman obsessed,
grabbing fistfulls of greens from saturated earth.
I pull up deep roots of dandelions. Satisfying.
Last fall I took a sledge hammer to that huge, craggy stump.
Whacked it into chunks that flew in all directions.
Now, a bowl of dirt brimming with lambs quarters
which I snatch and cast into a pile,
retrieving clumps of porous wood, a piece of petrified coal,
a rusty wire, a hinge without purpose.
I try to remember what stately tree stood here, next to
      the house
where my father, grandparents, and great grandparents lived.
White wooden siding, a screen porch that housed the christ-
      mas cactus in summer,
a sadly dissonant piano in a small living room,
the gas stove that shot up flames of gold, orange, green, blue
      in winter,
the sprawling kitchen with slanted floor of worn linoleum,
the cramped bedroom where grandma spent her last days
trying to fish a girl out of her cup with a spoon,
the steep stairs to grandpa's abode,
a narrow pallet, narrow room where snores rumbled
      with rafters.
Beyond that the big bedroom where a chamber pot nestled

beneath the high bed, where my cousin and I dared
to touch each other one night,
scared and amazed by pleasure not spoken.
The portrait of great grandma did not accuse
as her right eye and left eye were busy crossing themselves.
Large cedar trees caught armfuls of wind
while chickens roosted in the drafty wood barn.
Memories seep up inside with each fist of weeds until a circle
     of soil is empty.
There my husband and I will plant canterbury bells and
     trailing petunias
as maggots cling to wood lumps, earthworms burrow,
     ants crawl.
Earth made so soft by the tree that grew, died, decayed, then
     was gone.

Tree of Light

by Joy Pendleton
illustrated by Edenne Bowlby

A few years ago I was taking a walk along an old country road feeling full of light and love. So I talked and sang to the trees, plants, animals and birds I saw along the way. Such a nice walk and such good feelings! I felt at one with the Universe!

The road was interesting because some of it was paved, some was gravel, and some was clay. Some parts were very secluded, and it felt easier to "sing out" in those areas. One song I love to sing to nature is the "Sufi Blessing," which goes like this:

> *May the blessings of God rest upon you,*
> *May God's peace abide with you,*
> *May God's presence illuminate your heart,*
> *Now and forevermore!*

I stopped to sing this song to a tree in one of the secluded areas close to the road. I sang it loud with feeling, because no traffic was around, and because I was bursting with gratitude that morning. To my surprise, the tree lit up! When I sang, "May God's presence illuminate your heart," did it do just that? I gazed at it, startled, but honored beyond belief. I wanted to fall to my knees, and I felt like I was in another dimension. With tears in my eyes, I continued to gaze at the tree for a while after its light had faded away. I thanked the tree, so grateful for this unbelievable communication, turned and continued on my way.

To this day, my rational side wonders if the tree actually lit up—or did I see that in my mind's eye? It was one of those wonderful spiritual experiences that one hopes will happen again in this lifetime. I do feel the tree was reacting to my song (not being a good singer), and I will always believe that tree was thanking me for honoring it!

I will forever see trees differently. There is real love there. I see them as compassionate, majestic guardians.

This experience inspires me when I go out to feed the birds early in the morning while praying and singing to God, trees, birds, animals, insects, plants, rocks and soil, and nature spirits. I sing different songs: "O' Great Spirit," "Morning Has Broken," "Amazing Grace," etc. Sometimes I think the birds and squirrels would rather I just finish putting out the birdseed, but I do feel my songs of praise are understood, especially by those magnificent, mystical trees!

Namasté

If Trees Could Speak

by Carol Flake Chapman

In myth, the suffering or fearful turn into trees,
Suddenly rooted in their sorrow or their flight.
They must now turn to the sun for comfort.
Their hunger must now be satisfied from the soil.
They find themselves speechless until the wind
Rustles their leaves and gives them a voice.
In their new form, they send us a message.
We are not alone, they say. We are not afraid.
Because now we know what it is to be one
With the earth, the wind, the rain and the stars.
Because now we speak in the mother tongue.

Circle of Seven
Excerpt from Marisol's Dream

written and illustrated by Hollyana Melear

Much could be said about my love and relationship with trees. Trees have been many things to me: parents, teachers, listeners, companions, oracles...and not in the least, they have been my protectors. This is a story of the latter. It was not until an intimate situation with some very special trees in my life, that I was to become a true believer in a reciprocal relationship with nature. That is to say, I had always felt that Nature, the Great Mother, only listened, and perhaps if we were lucky, we received some small physically manifested gifts: a butterfly landing on us, or a bird flying over our head at just the right moment. This intimate event shaped my relationship to Earth and all aspects of the Great Mother. I would never look at Earth again as though she was not listening very intently to every word spoken.

As I begin this story, it seems to emerge like a strange metaphysical Grimm's fairy tale. Due to my way of thinking, and love of fairy tales, I will attempt to tell this story as such:

There once was a lovely and perfect forest. A young girl named Marisol lived nearby, and would often run into the woods to escape the urban constraints of her neighborhood, as well as the burdens of her family. She and her sister would often run there together. They found a back entrance into the woods, where Marisol would pretend like she was wandering down a forbidden path into a beautiful lair that gave her every-thing she desired.

This back entrance into the woods led Marisol to a partic-ularly magical place. Beside a stream there stood a circle of seven cedar and oak trees, standing on the northeast side of the forest. It seemed to have grown just for her, and had always been waiting for her. She would sit in the circle, and listen to the trees. Later, she would see what they saw—with their strange tree vision. The cedars' vision was a quick and flattened pulsation, almost like a short panoramic view. The colors in the cedars' vision were a bit muted and blurred together. Marisol felt a longing with this vi-sion; a desire to walk forward through a door, but she could not see any door. The oaks were quite different. Here, the vision pul-sated at a much slower pace; the contrast was sharper, and she did not feel the pull that she felt with the cedars.

When Marisol experienced this tree vision, her senses changed as well. The pressure seemed to change in the atmo-sphere, like it does before a big storm rolls in. Noise intensifies but quiets at the same time. She could hear bugs buzzing and chirp-ing. Bird calls echoed, and seemed far away. And there existed a quiet hum underlying everything. Everything seemed to slow down, as if she was moving through water. It was like the whole universe was patiently waiting for her, and saying, "Come on. It's okay. This is what is next."

Both types of trees, which filled the "Circle of Seven," made Marisol feel welcome. She formed a great bond with them, and would touch them and thank them. In the circle, she would pray, create drawings and write. Later, as an adult, she returned for comfort time and again. The woods would change through the years, but this space remained the same for the girl. In her twen-ties, she would bring men to the woods, and make love near the circle, but never within it. It was a sacred space that was solely for her and the trees. However, she felt extremely pulled to honor the "Circle of Seven," create within, and make love nearby. Mostly, she visited the circle by daylight, but sometimes she would return alone at night.

By and by, this pattern changed after Marisol had grown up, and lived with a partner named Joshua for several years. He was not a generous man. However, he was handsome, often idealistic, and she found things she loved in him greatly. Their love of nature was a common tie.

One night, she decided to bring him to her "Circle of Seven." They crept in the back way, and down to the northeastern side of the woods. They paused at a large rock in the middle of the stream, which she thought of as her altar. It was close to the Circle, but not within. There, as she and her partner began to make love, the pressure in the forest changed. Marisol had felt this before, but not in her woods. In haunted places, the pressure would change like this upon a visitation. She hated the feeling. Joshua often disagreed with her "musings" about seeing or feeling things that were not apparent in the physical world. This time, strangely, her skeptical partner also felt it.

As the pressure changed, the forest grew completely still. It must have been only seconds, but it was as if all of life, even the wind, stopped and held its breath. Marisol looked at Joshua, and they connected on a primal level of fear. Something very dark was coming. In those seconds, after they caught each other's eyes, a deep noise struck the ground from far away. She was reminded of the movie " Jurassic Park," and the scene where the T. rex made his first appearance. One could hear the rumble of his feet, and the whole ground shook. Within the woods, the deep vibration shook the forest.

It took only this first sound for them to be troubled by a deep recognition that the Dark was coming. As the second rumbling step sounded, Marisol and Joshua shook themselves, and frantically began to dress. The third step was so much closer to them. The Dark was coming for THEM. The steps got closer and faster, setting off panic.

A chase was about to be set in motion. As Joshua began to run, Marisol could feel the Dark direct its attention towards him. She started to run, as well, reaching the "Circle of Seven" in just a few steps. As she approached the circle, the trees spoke. They told her to stop, walk, and go slow. Fear only feeds.

Marisol called out to Joshua, telling him to come to her. He ran over, and she told him that they would never outrun it. They needed to walk very slowly out of the woods. Joshua looked at her as if she was crazy. This dark thing was clearly coming for them. Nonetheless, he agreed. Walk they did, and the Dark stalked immediately behind them.

They walked out of the woods that night. Back at their car, Joshua was confused and terrified. That night he had become a believer in other realms that exist along with us. Marisol was also scared, yet immensely grateful. The trees had spoken—and protected her. She knew that the Great Mother contained Shadow and Light, and she had mingled with both tonight, and had escaped with greater wisdom. In the future, she would always remember that the Earth would speak to her, if she listened. It was very important to honor the wisdom that Earth, the Great Mother, chose to share. More than that, she was honored that there was a witness. She would get many other confirmations from witnesses through the years. Every once in a while, when she would question herself and scream for her sanity, the Mother would gift her with certainties. It was a bountiful thing, and would only grow in intimacy over time.

As I have grown into adulthood—and a slow maturity that has been—I continue to learn about reciprocity. The gifts of the Great Mother are numerous, and my trust for Earth is great. I rely on Her communication in those private, still, and natural moments. However,

these last few years, I have begun to focus my attention on giving back. I breathe into the Earth my appreciation, by pulling energy from the cosmos into the Earth, for the Great Mother to redistribute to all lifeforms. Her giving is ceaseless, and never-ending is Her flow. There is always more than enough. Saying that, I know there is always more than enough for us to return to the world. It is the great gift—reciprocity between Heaven and Earth, allowing mankind to be a bridge for peace, love, and consciousness—and hopefully with plenty of joy prevailing upon the Earth.

Welcome Home

by Shiila Safer

Ho Grandmother Tree
we share life's breath
you and I
tied eternally
to the infinite

at the depths of my being
I breathe in your gift of life
thank you
for your generosity
your love
your breath

you know me at my core
closer to me
than I am to myself
guiding me to the deepest parts of me

I trust you
I trust me
I trust us together
we are a good team, you and I
for when we are together
I feel whole
a truth underlying all others
I feel a peace
rarely known at other times

you are a portal for me
when I step through your doorway
Oneness with All That Is
greets me on the other side
and welcomes me Home

The Mulberry Tree: Garden Of Eden?

by Will Taegel

illustrated by P. Cleve Ragan

O ne warm, autumn day in the Mideast, I approached a desert mulberry tree on the crest of a hill—a funny protrusion that looked a bit like the potbelly of a pig. The name of this unobtrusive hill is Göbekli Tepe, Turkish for said pig. Little did I know that conversations with this solitary tree would eventually shatter the lens through which I perceived the world. Trees have a way of upsetting our paradigms when we humans listen. Some day we may grow tails again as portrayed by the Na'vi in Avatar so that we can plug the tails into the trees and allow them to send us messages that can lead us into a new sense of equilibrium with the web of life all around us. Until then we can sit quietly with them and ask for their wisdom.

To set a context for my encounter with this mulberry tree and the importance of its particular landscape to the human narrative, journey with me to the aforementioned Göbekli Tepe in southeastern Anatolia in Turkey, about thirty miles from the Syrian border. Today, from the top of the hill, you can hear the bombs exploding in nearby villages across the border as the clash between human cultures accelerates into chaos. Although the bombs and extremists were not active when I was there, I can almost hear them as I return to the mulberry tree in my meditations. I wonder: do the solutions to our current planetary conundrums lie in the roots of our trees, the brain systems of plant intelligence reaching down to draw from the depths what we modern humans have forgotten? And is this particular tree pivotal?

Something seemed special about this particular tree, as if it was broadcasting packets of information from a distant past that reached through our confusion to a possible future. The mulberry tree's signals called a local Kurdish farmer to plow in its shade on a rather ordinary hot day at the edge of this desert wilderness nearly twenty years ago. His plow banged into a large stone. With tender hands he dusted off the top portion of the protrusion and was surprised to see it had ancient markings.

That simple moment of awareness and awakening by an alert farmer opened the door for archeologists to explore what some scientists are calling Earth's oldest temple and the dawn of human's earliest civilization. One archeologist I talked to while I was there speculated that it might be the original Garden of Eden.

Archeology keeps pushing the dates of our beginning civilizations back and back into the mists of human interaction. So much so that our very definitions of civilization are being challenged. Likewise, our understanding of human capabilities are being shaken. Questions arise such as: is it more civilized to fly drones and friend on facebook than to understand the messages of trees? Do trees have a vested interest in us even though we have traumatized them?

Dated at about 11–12,000 years ago, the discovery of Göbekli Tepe has turned the scientific and spiritual world upside down with such unsettling questions. To give you an idea of its age, the site contains human expressions thousands of years older than the Garden of Eden accounts recorded in Genesis, likely written about 1400 BCE. Or consider our much ballyhooed Stonehenge: this sacred site was likely built about 3000 BCE.

I draw these dates to our attention so that we can appreciate the gift of this little mulberry tree as it calls us beyond our Western Civilization paradigms by showing us that the building blocks of our culture are youngsters compared with Göbekli. We moderns have such a difficult challenge in reaching beyond the lenses we have been given to look at the human story. New discoveries keep providing us with different angles of perception.

For example, as I was writing this piece, an editor stated that the Garden of Eden as recorded in the Biblical account is "the greatest tree story ever told."

Maybe. Yet, this little tree seems to be calling us out of our habitual way of seeing the world and giving us an earlier and, perhaps, more basic tree story.

Perhaps, the tree has a story that transcends and yet includes the Biblical tree narratives?

Maybe, it seeks to introduce us to a new relationship with the circle of life after we estranged ourselves from the mysterious life cycle through our own desire to dominate the natural order rather than live humbly as a specie among species.

Maybe, the tree attempts to call us into a shared partnership rather than a paternal stewardship where we assume we are the pennacle of evolution.

Maybe, the tree can assist us in being collaborators in the garden rather that fatherly stewards, a practice that seems to lead us to trashing the garden.

With these jolting reflections on my mind, I climbed to the summit of the hill overlooking the astonishing dig to sit beneath the aforementioned mulberry tree. The tattered strips of prayer cloth placed on the tree by local Sufis—a mystical and generally progressive wing of Islam—reminded me of colorful strips of cloth hanging from branches of a juniper tree on our land back in the Texas Hill Country. These flags blow in the wind and point the way to a sweat lodge, or, as we say in tribal language, "inipi." "Inipi" translates to place of spirits or energies—a description that also fits this sacred site in Turkey. The stones we utilize in the sweat lodge ceremony seem to connect me with Göbekli and the magnificent slabs rising out of the ground 20 feet tall and weighing 20 tons.

Now, with this background I am prepared to tell you how the mulberry tree at Göbekli turned my world upside down. The grandson of the Kurdish farmer, who was drawn to this bleak eco-field to bring prayer flags to the tree, sat beside me as a new friend and guide. We both leaned against the trunk of the tree. The grandson told me how the tree itself transmitted information about the site and how the people whose art graced the area were speaking to us today if we could only translate. The tree, he explained, sent information to him that was far more insightful than the musings of German archeologists now heading the dig. After our conversation descended into silence, my new friend wisely left me to be alone with the tree.

The wind whistled through the limbs. Small, brown birds hopped nearby pecking at the berries. I closed my eyes and, belatedly, asked permission to be there. Like most Westerners, I had just blundered in and assumed I could lean against the tree.

More silence ensued. Then, wordless words came up through the roots and passed through my body as if through an electromagnetic field, and a narrative unfolded.

Here is what I heard from the tree as it transmitted not only its own wisdom but also information and meaning arising from the matrix of systemic eco-fields in which it grew. The language was strange to my inner ear as it mixed with my psychological projections. I have elsewhere called the language used in the communication, the mother tongue. Not being fluent in this primordial transmission inhibits my ability to share with you; nevertheless, here it is.

"I am the granddaughter of the tree of knowledge, many generations removed from your stories about Eden. I carry in my cells the memories of a first man and a first woman who lived as respectful companions, intimate with themselves and us. They were unashamed of their nakedness, surrounded by us trees. We were pleasing to the eye and offered good food for them.

"Humans listened to us and noticed how we provided them with fruit. I heard the humans interpret God's mind, warning of the potential curse of a sedentary life centered on possessions. I watched with grief as I saw you humans leave behind a life of hunting and gathering. As roving children of the Earth you could move with responsiveness to changing conditions. As children of Earth you worked a couple of hours a day and sought deeper life and recreation the rest of the time. Yet, you chose to fix yourselves, domesticate, proliferate, and store up wealth. I grieved your absence from sitting and listening to me and my sisters as you toiled behind the plow sunup to sundown with your new found skill of making gardens of the land.

"I saw you lose your physical height, shrinking a good six inches in stature. Why even the people who live around me today have not regained the height of their hunter-gatherer ancestors. Even though you, Will, are near six feet tall, you are shorter than the ancient sculptors of this place. I saw humans imagine they were progressing, as early farmers, in the new-found power of agriculture—only to cultivate more anemia, vitamin deficiencies, a shorter lifespan, weak teeth, spinal deformity, and rampant infectious diseases, while living in closer proximity to other humans and livestock. First you created fixed villages, then cities, then nations. I saw you humans multiplying with increasing numbers, while harmfully reducing us trees to a small percentage of what Earth needs. Will, this is what I saw about your human story."

The wind rustles through the branches of the little tree. Her mood changes as she continues to speak to me in the present tense to emphasize the gist of what she wants me, maybe us, to grasp.

"When will you return to me? When will you become part of my forests? When will you give me at least as much attention as you direct to computers and shopping malls? I miss you. We all miss you."

I had no ready response to the mulberry tree. Or to thoughts I projected into the conversation with the tree, as I tried to sort valid information from what might have been my imagination. When I did not reply with specific answers to the tree, the tree seemed patient but insistent.

Even now, I stumble at legitimate objections to the call to return to the cycle of life. Humans in my seminars and my colleagues will often come at me hard—accusing me of ignoring the gifts of Leonardo, Michelangelo, and Mozart—as well as air-conditioning, rubber-soled shoes, and iPads. I know. I know, I say. We can't go back, only forward. We don't even know if the Göbekli people were hunter gatherers or farmers or urbanites or some civilization beyond our grasp.

I've had few responses to these insistent questions, only more questions, both for my fellow humans and for this lovely tree. I experienced a profound sense of loss and ignorance as I sought to recover an intimacy of conversation with my new acquaintance, the mulberry tree. Not having rational responses to the tree or to valid questions raised by friends and paradigmatic foes, I breathed and returned to the mother tongue for respite.

I ran my hands over the tree's bark, caressing. Part of me felt hurried to leave the tree, and look at the stone sculptures, human creations. A deeper aspect within implored me to stay next to the tree. I noticed serrated leaves with dots of brown. On the ground were dried up red berries or were they black? I could not tell. I held the berries and thought of jams, wines, and breakfast.

I knew that green versions of the fruit were used as an entheogen, most likely by the hunter-gatherers, to evoke visions around their ceremonial fires. I longed to know the secrets of the plant and to allow its medicine to course through my blood, grounding me yet sending me to new heights. I imagined the taste of its sacrament to be earthy in my mouth, giving me a slight numbness.

I looked to the blue sky and the searing sun above. Light streamed through the leaves; faint hints of Black Elk's childhood vision of the cottonwood tree pirouetted across my mind's screen. Images of ancients took shape before me, as if called forth by my touch of the green bark. Some ancient psychopharmacology coursed through my veins made possible not by ingestion but by light touch.

Later, I found out that the bark is the sole food of the silk worm and, in that sense, this tree has bequeathed humans all things silk. Who would know? I discovered that this little tree is full of practical medicine, even a cure for ringworm, a skin fungus. I know that trees everywhere gift us with medicine. I know they breathe, and without this tree, and its friends throughout the planet, I could not take a single breath.

The little mulberry tree, the tree of knowledge, was patient and quiet, intimate in its nourishment. I looked at the circle of sculpted megaliths. I became aware that these Göbekli ancients opened the door to the modern world, so long ago. I shifted on the hard ground and was aware that the discomfort was not only my sit bone but also a glaring fact: an elephant in the middle of the room. We humans have wandered far off into an abstract and now virtual world. In the name of objectivity and critical thinking, we have set ourselves apart from the rest of creation, as if we belong more to the gods than the manifest world, itself divine.

Once again the tree spoke to me, "You humans are at a fork in the road. We invite you back into the circle of life. Despite all that you have done to desecrate, we open our arms to you."

Fumbling into my backpack, I took a metal bottle of water, poured an offering on the roots, and replied, "I am not sure I know the way back to the circle, but I resolve to know you and your kind better. I don't know the way for a return. I don't know your mother tongue or even if I am just imagining this conversation. Our grandfather, Black Elk, wondered if there was life left in the roots of the tree of life, but I hear you wondering if there is life left in us humans. The only gift I seem to have as I wind my way into the sacred cycle is my willingness. Will you show me the direction? Will you be my mentor?"

Adapted from *The Mother Tongue: Intimacy in the Eco-field* by Will Taegel.

Messages and Meditations

Trees are sanctuaries. Whoever knows how to speak to them, whoever knows how to listen to them, can learn the truth. They do not preach learning and precepts, they preach undeterred by particulars, the ancient law of life.

Hermann Hesse

Circular Breathing Practice

by Shiila Clear Tree

I'd like to share with you a simple breathing practice that Grandmother Oak taught me one morning.

- Get comfortable with your tree (find a position where you can relax).
- As you breathe in, say to yourself "I breathe in what you breathe out".
- Really focus and feel it.
- When you breathe out, say " I breathe out what you breathe in" and feel that.
- As you settle into breathing in this way, give thanks to your 'breathing partner'.
- Feel the rhythm of your symbiotic relationship.
- Really feel the circle of reciprocity.
- Notice how your body feels.
- Give gratitude and say goodbye when you are ready to move on to something else.

It's an intimate moment when you breathe with someone. You will notice your relationship with the trees deepen as you do this breathing practice over time. We all do it all the time; the difference here is bringing your awareness to your breath and shifting from unconscious breathing to conscious breathing in relationship with the Tree People, who give us life.

From the Trees

through Wendy Grace

Welcome to our conversation, to our thousand eyes and ears,
      to our consciousness
We are one being and we are aware of our nature this way
So when one of us is cut down it is a part of our body
And that part, that one, contains the whole
This is the sacred nature of life.
We know this and we can grow very close to each other,
We know each others' memories so we remember all things

Some of us don't grow to our full heights before
Our bodies return to the earth
To enter life anew
Yet every part of us no matter how small
Knows all that is given to us to know
That knowing feeds life, roots life on this planet
The most exquisite dance of elements, of sky and expansion
And of earth and rock and density
At the edge, the interface of earth and sky we grow...

This is how you are and you do not know it yet,
Having locomotion and an exploration of individuality
      and uniqueness...
In your next stage of life you will be aware of this connectedness
This oneness and you will know who you are
So anything you do to anyone else you do to yourself
Awareness of this opens the most exquisite intimacy and song

A world of acceptance and allowing
Beyond the judgment of right and wrong
Know yourselves and to whom you belong forever
This miraculous continuum of life....

Redwood, Madrone, Bay, Oak, Tan Oak, Fir—this was a united voice
Santa Cruz, California, 2007

Listening with Your Whole Body

by Shiila Safer

This is an exercise in quieting the mind and opening the senses; in feeling rather than thinking.

Trust the wisdom of your body. We are experimenting with direct communication with trees/plants/Earth, without words, concepts or pre-conceived notions. Open your listening.

- Feel yourself called to a particular tree, flower or plant in the garden.
- Stand barefoot next to it, opening the connection with your K1 kidney acupuncture point† in the bottom of your feet and the Earth.
- Even if you are not barefoot, continue with the practice, as you will feel the connection with the tree or plant through your hands
- Hold open your hands over or next to the tree or plant, palms facing it.
- Quiet your mind by focusing on your breath.
- Bring your attention to your hands and feel the energy in your hands.
- Notice what you notice.
- Is there tingling or pulsing?

---

† Activating the Chinese medicine point called "The Bubbling Spring" will send a "Spiral of Power" through your entire body. This is because when you connect the K1 Kidney Acupuncture point to the earth, it unleashes one of the most powerful anti-aging secrets ever. It's a super way to "wake up" your feet!" (http://www.gettoyourcore.com/bubbling-spring/)

- Do you feel you are making an energetic connection with the tree or plant? Stand there for a few minutes; it may take a while to feel this.

- Bring your attention to your feet.

- Notice what you notice.

- Do you feel a tingling or pulsing?

- Can you feel your connection with the Earth?

- Now see if you sense or feel a circle of energy pulsing through your body.

- Earth, feet, hands, tree or plant. Or, tree or plant, hands, feet, Earth and back again.

- Can you feel the energy moving with your body as a conduit?

- Breathe into your heart and out of your heart as you stand in the stream of life force energy from Earth to tree/plant and back again.

- Open to receiving any insights or messages that may come to you.

- Allow your heart message to be sent.

- Offer your gratitude for this Earth blessing, knowing that this gift is always available to you.

- Say 'goodbye' and 'thank you' in your own way to the tree/plant before you break the connection.

Words of Wisdom
From Grandmother Oak

through Shiila Clear Tree

Each day when you climb up and sit in my branches, you feel the stillness in your own being. You attribute it to me. You access wisdom and teachings which you also attribute to me. It's as if I act as a high-powered mirror showing you what you might otherwise not be able to see.

What makes information available to us? The fine tuning device of our bodies; our physical, mental, emotional and energetic bodies. When you sit with me, you can tune in more effectively than at other times and places. We co-create an open learning environment. Without judgment we explore the places where your curiosity is leading you. We open to the wisdom of the trees, the insects, the birds, Earth and Sky. We open to the Timeless Now.

I provide a safe container and grounding for your journeys. You can depend on me to be here, unconditionally accepting and loving. It's important for you to remember that you bring your willingness, your trust, and your love, without which our time together would be very superficial.

Have patience with yourself. You are learning a new language. Every one of your senses is used in union with this form of communication. The "Mother Tongue," as you are calling it, is inside your being—in your cells, and at the same moment, both hidden and accessible. At any moment you can tune in and open your receptors to receive the vibration, and information will be delivered to you. At every moment, you are transmitting your information to the universe.

As you become more transparent, you feel less resistance and separation. Opening is the key. Traveling on the breath is your path. The breath is the vehicle into both inner and outer space.

Although you may wonder if you're really getting anything—or feeling the energy—you are. You are also demonstrating a willingness to open, to practice, to learn this new language that is your birthright as a living being on Earth. This language that has been so covered up, and has now been rediscovered, named, and brought to your attention—this is your practice. This is your path. This is your discovery. This is your work. This is your passion and your longing.

You could string together the most memorable and powerful moments of your life, and give them this name—"Mother Tongue Intimacy." (*Taegel, 2012*)

Increasingly, people are waking up their ability to communicate with trees and other relations. It is time. It is what's being called for. Earth, herself, is calling humans to join the living community of active intelligence, once again.

As humans take their place among the community of active intelligence, the dynamics will shift and Earth will thrive. As it is now, humans are a drain on Earth's energy and resources. This needs to stop. It is time to embrace your fellow Travelers on Earth (more-than-humans) as equals, as intelligent life with wisdom to share. There is much for you to learn from each other.

It is essential today for women to feel their connectedness with the Earth. Women are, after all, vessels through which life force flows. In their day-to-day activities, very few women are consciously aware of this vital connection.

Women, NOW is the time. Take a few moments every day to ground yourselves in the Earth, to send your roots down into Mother's rich soil. Lean up against a tree and invite the tree to assist you in making this connection more tangible for you. Ask for help and you will receive it. Just think of how much more energy you will have when you access the Earth's abundant life force! This generous gift is always available to you, although you do need to consciously align yourself with it in order to fully benefit.

We are being asked to make the final jump from connection
    to oneness.
From aspiring to being. It takes opening, letting go, conscious
    choice, surrender.
Walk together into a new day—a new way of being human.
A new way of carrying Earth energy in your being.
Conscious recognition of essence.
Walk in that awareness and choose to live that way.
Binding structures do not easily fall away, as they put up a
    good fight.
It takes courage and trust to stand in your own truth and move
    forward in an entirely new direction.
Earth is asking each of us to do just that.
To move forward with her—to consciously merge with her energy
    field as One Being—thus strengthening the field.

Humans need to draw on the strength and synergy of community. As communities come together in love and light, opening to the guidance of Spirit and Earth, a field is strengthened on Earth.

The more these communities are consciously choosing Earth as their mother—as their core, as their essence, as their teacher, as themselves—the more Earth herself is strengthened, nourished, balanced and whole. Many children split off from her, and separation has taken its toll. Creation is ongoing. Life force is constant. Humans are evolving.

Using the breath is the key, like unlocking the door to other realms. Follow the breath and it will take you on journeys beyond your wildest imagination.

Use the breath as a teacher, a guide, a tool, a point of awareness, an object of meditation.

The mystery of the breath holds the mystery of the universe and of our creation.

If we could only glimpse the information carried by the breath into and out of our physical bodies—the communication from Spirit to every cell in our bodies, and every particle of our being.

This time is crucial for humans, as you know. It is imperative that our wisdom be shared with as many humans as possible. Now is a critical time. There is more energy, light, and awareness available now than ever before in human history. There is also more destruction and disconnection than ever before.

It is a choice for the human race. People need to be educated. That is where you come in. You are a teacher and can educate people in the ways of reconnecting with us and other Earth Teachers. Support is needed at every level, no matter how simple. People need help. I will continue to feed you information through your physical body and your experience. You can benefit from the research of others, but it is only in your own experience that you come to a place of knowing.

I stand tall and my arms open to Sky. Wisdom floats on Air and Wind and rustles my branches, whispering to the leaves, bringing me news from far places.

Earth feeds me information that flows through me. My human friends open their minds to me, and heart wisdom is transferred and shared between us. I learn from every meeting with every bird, squirrel, ant, and human.

I am available for information exchange. Energy flows freely from my brothers and sisters in the tree community; we help each other to grow, and we protect other living creatures.

We guard sacred places.
We hold the energy for whomever can feel it and benefit from it.
We teach stillness.
We offer peace.
We love playing with children.
We offer protection and safety.
We hold libraries of information.

We offer our wisdom in collaboration with humans for the benefit of Earth. It's time to listen. We have so much to say. Every human who thinks they hear us, do hear us. Every human who feels our presence discovers who we are. Every human who touches us, is touched in return.

Grandmother Oak
Texas Live Oak
Wimberley, Texas, 2012, 2013

Being Breathed by the Tree

by Shiila Clear Tree

This is a step-by-step version of the meditation practice described in the story, *Breathed by Tree*. Experiment with it and see what happens for you!

- Identify a favorite tree, either one that you have established a relationship with, or one that calls to you now.
- Approach the tree and ask it if you may get close and touch it.
- When you feel invited in, find a comfortable position where you can physically touch the tree at one or more of the connection points; with the palms of your hands, the bottom of your feet, your root chakra at the base of the spine, your heart chakra in the center of your chest (also felt through the center of your back), your third eye chakra in the center of your forehead, or your crown chakra on the top of your head.
- Position yourself, relax and focus on your breath.
- Get comfortable. Settle in.
- Breathe into your heart and out of your heart.
- Do this for a while, until your mind settles and you feel a connection with the tree.
- Ask the tree if she/he will breathe you.
- Surrender your breath to the tree, letting go of control of your breathing (this is very subtle).
- Without engaging your mind in the process, clearly hold your intent to be breathed by the tree.
- See what happens. Let go.
- Notice what you notice.

- This is hard to describe in words, it's more of a feeling state. It also may take some practice.
- Is your energy connected with the energy of the tree?
- It is in this state of intimate connection that you may receive downloads of information from the tree. Is there a message for you?
- This is a two-way communication; open to transmitting information to the tree as well (through images, feelings, and/or words).
- When you feel complete, give thanks to the tree and say 'goodbye' before breaking the connection.

The information you receive will be stored in your body for future reference, so don't be concerned if you cannot remember it all. Also, your exchange with the tree may be primarily an energetic exchange without words, deep and enriching. Know also that the trees have made it known to us that they are grateful for this practice, and available for intimate connection with humans. You may choose to make this one of your regular practices. If you do, it is your gift to the trees.

Returning

through Shiila Safer

returning
it's time for returning
come back into relationship with us
over these many years
humanity has recognized me for my size
there has been a thread of connection that has been broken

it's time to return to our common roots
you are children of life itself, as am I
with access to wisdom beyond your years
knowledge transmitted through the web of connection
through the web of life

you tell me your stories
can you open to mine?

Great Grandmother
860-year-old Montezuma Bald Cypress
Utopia, Texas, 2013
3rd largest tree in Texas

Wind in the Trees Meditation

by Shiila Safer

On a delightfully windy day, find yourself a tree that will invite you in. This meditation can be done in a variety of ways. Either climb up into the tree and find a comfortable spot for sitting or standing, stand on the ground leaning up against the tree and looking up, or lie on your back on the ground beneath the tree.

- Find a comfortable spot with your tree.
- Take a slow deep breath and begin to relax.
- Ask the tree for permission to join with it in a new way.
- Once you feel welcomed, notice your body relax even further.
- Open to a spacious sense of self. Be willing to let go of your normal solid sense of who you are and experiment with becoming the tree.
- On the exhale of another deep breath, send your own roots down into the ground, to mix with the roots of the tree. If you are standing, feel these roots extend down through the bottom of your feet. If you are sitting, extend them through the base of your spine. If you are lying down, then reach down into the Earth from your belly.
- As you continue to breathe slowly, consciously let your breath take you down into your roots.
- Feel your body ground with the tree, strong and stable, solidly in the Earth.
- Now, with your roots solidly planted in the rich soil, bring your attention back up from your roots into your body, slowly feeling the connection.
- Notice your new sense of rootedness.

- From this place of grounded connection, bring your awareness to the top of the tree, to the branches swaying in the wind and the leaves dancing.
- Reach your arms up the trunk of the tree to rest on the branches if you can, or simply reach up towards them. If you are lying down, open your arms wide.
- If you are sitting up in the tree, be sure you are safe in your position.
- Imagine that your arms are the branches of the tree, your fingers the leaves.
- Reach for the sky.
- You are the tree, rooted in the Earth and reaching for the Sky.
- Feel the wind caressing you.
- See if you can let go of your usual sense of control and allow yourself to be moved by the wind.
- The wind is blowing your hair. It is the branches and leaves creaking, dancing, and flowing.
- Your skin feels the touch of the wind. Is it cool, or warm? How does it feel?
- You hear the wind whispering in your ears. What is it saying to you?
- Your arms are open wide, open to the sky. Feel your chest opening, your heart chakra (energy center) opening even further. Take a moment to notice how this feels.
- Allow the wind to move in you and bring spaciousness into your body.
- Be aware of any fragments of thoughts or images that may be rustled up by the wind.
- Notice if there is emptiness in your mind/body as the wind clears out old remnants of energies that you are ready to let go of.

- Make a mental note of how this feels.
- What other life forms are enjoying you as the tree?
- Are birds landing in your branches and singing?
- Are butterflies flitting by?
- Do they have any messages for you?
- Do you feel a sense of interconnectedness with the Nature Beings?
- Are you able to touch, even for a moment, what feels like your essence, your soul?
- Take a moment to rest in this space.
- Taking a slow, deep breath, thank the tree for hosting you so generously.
- Pulling your roots back up out of the ground, and your arms down from the tree, bring your awareness back into your physical body.
- Feel your own center, just below your belly.
- Take a nice, slow, deep breath from this place.
- Notice how your body feels now. What message does it have for you?
- Pick up a pen or pencil with your non-dominant hand, and capture, if you can, some of your awareness during the meditation. Think back, how did it feel to be the tree, waving your arms in the wind? Were there any messages from the wind, sky, tree, birds, butterflies, or your body?
- Write whatever arises in your mind, without editing. Feel the spaciousness of Sky as you write. Let the words flow easily through you.

Cypress Whispers

through Shiila Safer

I carry the energy and wisdom of the feminine Earth Mother expressing through trees. My roots reach down to the very core of life itself—the living waters of the river. The intricate web of life forms in Earth—soil, rock: granite, limestone. I intertwine my roots with my family of trees around me. We share resources and information, energy and life force. I nourish and nurture life.

The wind blows and my branches dance with information from the field. I hold the soil in place. I help create, along with my family, a stable riverbank. I provide stability and protection for you and squirrels, woodpeckers, and countless insects whose lives are interconnected with mine.

I am fluid
I am flexible
I am strong
I am stable
I am a bridge between Earth and Sky
As are you
My roots in the darkness of the womb of creation
My trunk carries the heart of Earth to be made visible to all beings
My branches reach to the vastness of Sky open to the whispers of
    the waves of possibilities
I give humans the air you breathe
We are breathing partners inextricability woven together in this
    dance of life

Take the time to listen. Feel how our lives are being threatened. It is difficult to see, but I feel it on the wind. The delicate balance of the interconnected web of life is being disrupted.

The trees have been charged with the protection of humans. Throughout time and the beginnings of civilization we have had a very special relationship with one another. Reach out to us now in this time of crisis. We are here to help you return to the web of life.

Grandmother Cypress
Blanco River
Wimberley, Texas, 2015

Message from the Oak Tree at Uisneach

through Tara Khandro

Uisneach, an approximately 8,000-year-old sacred site, is located in County Westmeath, Ireland. Uisneach lies at the exact center of the island, and is considered a portal, or "Sidhe," transporting visitors into the multidimensional "Other World."

All of the sacred trees of Ireland are represented at Uisneach. It is a powerful place of earth alchemy.

Two oak trees create a natural entryway onto the 2km that comprises Uisneach. One of the oak trees has grown a natural burl wide enough to comfortably sit upon. Judging from how smooth the burl is, it feels as if many people have taken a seat to contemplate the beginning of their journey into, essentially, the timeless space of the present moment.

I sit upon the burl, close my eyes and immediately hear the voice of this ancient wise oak. A gentle, strong, deep voice tells me, "Unity is the way to Be. Drop your false concepts of doing and not doing. Root yourself into the heart of Eriu (earth). Be the tree that you are. Rise up in faith that Heaven always has your best interest at heart. Feel your heart. Bring your head to meet your heart. Unity prevails."

Oak
Uisneach, County Westmeath, Ireland

Redwoods Speak

through Shiila Safer

Sit in stillness. Listen with your heart. This act of connection and respect is what is called for at this time. Bring all of your frustration, wisdom, sadness, and love into your point of connection with me. Know that I can feel you in all of your truth. Know also that we have been waiting for you to BE with us in this way.

All of your feelings of helplessness in the face of the Earth's current crisis can be surrendered in moments like this, to be replaced with relationship and connection. There are moments when action is needed and that action needs to be grounded in this deep level of connection.

It is your task in the world to foster and model a gentle loving reconnection with Earth Mother, trees and living waters. Remember how intertwined we are—trees and humans. Learn from us about community. Learn from us about truly nourishing one another. Learn from us about how to carry your strength and truth into the world.

Notice how many life forms each one of us support. Our lives are for the greater whole. We offer ourselves to you to teach you the deepest love, friendship, collaboration, surrender, and cooperation. Every life form depends on every other.

We invite you to stand up, speak out, become active. Continue to bring together community. Our song is stronger when we sing together. Our voices are more likely to be heard.

Redwoods
Mill Valley, California, 2015

A Message from an Ancient Sycamore

through Samarah Gabriel Grace

Greetings. What I would offer is that there are no lesser lights. Each pattern of creation has an intrinsic value that is to be recognized and nourished. You admire me because I have grown large and yet had you seen me as a young sapling, would you have been as lavish in your praise?

That which you dismiss or criticize or make light of or try to extinguish will rise up in rebellion and soon nature will be at odds with you. Instead, open to each atom of creation as if it was a newborn babe. Cradle it, rock it, sing to it and let there be a place for each of us and for all of us. Let us live in harmony and appreciation for all of creation. This is the song of praise I would most love to hear.

Sycamore
Montezuma's Well, Arizona, 2015

Closing Reflections

To all humans I send this invitation: let's return to the natural order and allow Mother Earth to restore us and redeem us from our destructive and exploitive behaviors. She is capable of magnificent and beautiful rebalancing, even of the likes of humans gone astray for the last 7000 years.

Will Taegel

An Invitation

by Shiila Safer

We invite you to be an ongoing participant in the expanding worldwide community of people who love trees. Thank you to all of you who came together in such a powerful way to support the publication of this beautiful book! As one of our contributors said to me, "It feels as though the trees of the world are connecting with one other." It does feel like that! The energy is palpable. The new connections that have been established in the process of bringing this book to publication will continue to grow, as the roots of trees spread both deep and wide across Mother Earth.

We remind you that you are not alone in your experiences of deep connection and communication with trees and with the Earth herself. One thing I have learned, while compiling this book, is that for human beings an intimate connection with trees is as universal as watching the stars. It's as natural as a child reaching out to its mother. Across time, cultural lines, age, and gender, there exists a deep mutual exchange between humans and trees. We invite you to explore that connection for yourself. Open to it. Remember your own stories.

Then we encourage you to deepen that connection and communication with trees and all of life, recognizing the reciprocal nature of our greater Universe. Notice how when we extend our energy of intent, and requests for help, the Universe often responds—sometimes very directly through synchronicities: a confluence of events or opportunities that come our way at just the right moment, giving us the feeling that our prayers have been answered.

One way to view trees is as supreme tuning devices channeling intelligence from the greater Universe—the energy fields beyond our manifest world. When we humble ourselves and open our senses and lines of communication with trees, we benefit from their generosity, their wisdom, and the intelligence of the Universe itself.

I feel it is essential for us to cultivate this open channel of communication now, because it offers a possibility for guidance from our intelligent ancestors, the Tree People, to reinstate balance and a healthy relationship with Earth and our natural world. Due to our long separation as a culture, we do not know how to go about this immense task. The wisdom that comes through the trees, and many of our brothers and sisters in this book, indicates a path that we are invited to walk as we find our way back home to wholeness, harmony, and balance.

I feel a sense of urgency in delivering the messages in this book. The trees encourage me; egg me on. *Intimacy with Trees* is a co-creation between humans and trees. The time is NOW. There is so much love, wisdom, and guidance available to us through the trees. It's as if they made an agreement at the beginning of time to assist humanity with our evolution of consciousness. They are calling us back into the web of life. It is time for The Great Return of humans to the cycle of life. Are we listening?

Have you had a moment of intimacy with a tree? Do you remember hugging a tree? Or leaning your back against a tree and daydreaming? Or feeling protected by a tree? What is your story? We invite you to share your story on our 2nd Tier Publishing website and/or Facebook page, and join the growing community of Tree Lovers who are actively practicing communication with the more-than-human world. We want to get to know you! We welcome you into our global community.

Intimacy with Trees is a small piece of a much bigger puzzle. It's the manifestation and expression of love and connection from many people around the world sharing their stories about trees. It is also a gift of love from the trees themselves—and a plea. In the bigger picture, it is a visible step in re-establishing an ongoing reciprocal relationship of co-creation, and returning to our innate connection with nature. We can resume our ability to communicate with trees by remembering the wonderful comfort of an intimate relationship with nature we experienced as children, and bringing from it the benefit of expanded awareness as adults.

Let's use *Intimacy with Trees* as a catalyst for ongoing direct experience. A seed, once planted, that continues to grow and flourish and reproduce. A loving memory, that once rekindled, deepens and permeates your being each time it is touched. In this way, we let the trees know that we are returning to the cycle of life, and that we are listening.

"Fortunately, like most children, I had learned what is most valuable, most indispensable for life before school years began, taught by apple trees, by rain and sun, river and woods ..."

Herman Hesse

About the Writers and Artists

With immense gratitude we introduce you to our contributing writers and artists who generously share their love for trees and heartfelt experiences with you.

Sheila Armitage

Sentinal Inviting: My Wise Friend, author

Sheila Armitage was born a nature lover. She has a deep relationship with trees, plants, hills, rocks, water, and wildlife, and their intelligent inter-relationships. Sheila is a happiness coach who partners with horses and nature, and combines neuroscience to open possibilities.

Sheila@TheWindhorseJourney.com

www.TheWindhorseJourney.com

Carol Bennington

Lilac's Lessons, author

Carol Bennington, PhD, is a flower essence practitioner, instructor and scholar, who has loved trees since birth.

Journey@Awakening-Hearts.com

www.Awakening-Hearts.com

Deborah Doblado Bowers, Two Trees Birthing

The Tree of Many Voices, author

Deborah Doblado Bowers is a tuning device. Her work flows in and out. Come into her vision space and see what it's all about.

deborahttb@icloud.com

Edenne Bowlby

Tree of Light, illustrator

Edenne Bowlby is a self-taught 17-year-old artist that lives to draw and draws to live.

ezbows@UseYourPowersForGood.com

Karina Konupek Bowlby
A Creation Story, illustrator

Karina Konupek Bowlby is a life-long artist continuously learning—blending intuition, symbolism and self expression.

art@byKarina.com
www.byKarina.com

R.Maya Briel
stories: *A Creation Story, Oledas,* and *Tree School*

In her own quest for connection and wholeness, R.Maya Briel dedicates herself to the ancient wisdom of Nature and Earth within.

Sharon Gwen Carter
The Loving Nature of Anticipation, author and illustrator
illustrations: *Gifts From Trees, Soul Retrieval in the Apple Orchard*
and *Intimacy with Trees* book cover
Intimacy with Trees book editor

Sharon Carter has had a productive career as nationally showcased illustrator, cartoonist, muralist, painter, and weaver. BFA from the University of Texas; certified as an art teacher in Hawaii; 35 years in the publishing industry. She is known in Wimberley, Texas as painter of the city's Rock Wall mural.

www.SharonGwenCarter.com

Carol Flake Chapman
If Trees Could Speak, poet

Carol Flake Chapman, whose most recent book is *Written in Water: A Memoir of Love, Death and Mystery*, lives in the hills west of Austin, Texas.

www.WrittenInWaterMemoir.com

Quaglia Cocco, Juliett Jade Chi

the olive tree, poet

Quaglia Cocco (Quail Coconut) is a citizen of Damanhur, spiritual eco-community in northern Italy, where she journeys through realms of expression and beauty every day, practices Damanhurian Sacred Dance as a spiritual path, and facilitates communications and storytelling with the world through the Damanhur Blog online presence.

quaglia@Damanhur.it

www.jadequail.wordpress.com

Peggy Cole

The Climbing Tree, author

Peggy Cole lives in Wimberley, Texas with horses, dogs, cats, and the wild world while enjoying a number of creative endeavors in service to the Earth (writing, photography, spirit groups, and helping farmers and ranchers succeed in a sustainable way).

PeggyrCole@gmail.com

Marlan Curry, Healing Juniper

The Big Oak Tree, author

Marlan Curry is complicated, silly, a bit shy, and love is his default mode.

Cathy Dyer

Compassionate Embrace: A Story of Co-Counseling with Trees, illustrator

Cathy Dyer is an artist and educator exploring and loving nature.

cdyer1018@gmail.com

Cheryl Elms

illustrations: *A Tribute to the Mighty Oak, The Tree of Many Voices, The Climbing Tree, Tree Love, Ancestral Trees, Li'l Boab,* and *Time is Stilled in These Ancient Groves*

Cheryl Elms is a full time mixed media artist who has exhibited nationally and who has been inspired to create art since her first drawings on the walls beside her crib.

elmzart@hotmail.com

www.elmzart.com

Laurel Emrys

Compassionate Embrace: A Story of Co-Counseling with Trees, author

Laurel Emrys is a professional musician (flute, harp, and voice) whose focus is the art and science of sound-healing through private sessions and group programs, called *Being In Harmony.*

Info@LaurelEmrys.com

www.BeingInHarmony.us

www.LaurelEmrys.com

Oberto Airaudi, "Falco"

untitled poems

Philosopher, painter, healer, poet and writer Falco, Oberto Airaudi (1950–2013), the inspiration and Spiritual Guide of Damanhur, Federation of Community. Falco had awakened in himself the capacity to tap into the great reservoirs of knowledge of our universe. His work brought to life a new spiritual paradigm, new arts and sciences.

federation@Damanhur.it

www.Damanhur.info

Wynn Renee Freeland

Ancestral Trees, author

Wynn Renee Freeland, former psychotherapist, singer, songwriter, poet, dynamic dreamer.

Miranda Gibson

Observer Tree in Tasmanian Forest, author

Miranda Gibson is an environmental activist who has dedicated many years to living in and fighting to defend Australia's precious native forests.

www.ObserverTree.org

Ashe Godfrey

Falling Leaves, poet
Li'l Boab, author

Ashe Godfrey is a "mum" of 5, living in the beautiful historic town of Jarrahdale, Western Australia surrounded by trees—and wouldn't have it any other way.

Samarah Gabriel Grace

A Message from an Ancient Sycamore, messenger

Samarah Gabriel Grace is a conscious channel for Mother Mary as well as a writer, minister and spiritual guide.

www.ChannelMary.com

Wendy Grace
Tree Love, author
From the Trees, messenger

Wendy Grace, an artist and environmental activist with an extensive background in alternative healing, explores a close relationship with Nature and has been an active friend of Damanhur for many years. Wendy is a key co-creator of the Global Tree Network, a global campaign of awareness and celebration of the relationship between humans and trees.

www.GlobalTreeNetwork.com

Bruce P. Grether
poetry: *The Secret Language of Leaves* and *The Holy Book of Trees*

Bruce P. Grether grew up in Thailand, and in Berkeley, California during the 1960s; he is a Wizard who has published many books and offers workshops.

www.9realities.com

Gurutej
Tree Hugging Cactus, author

Gurutej lives the meaning of her Sikh name (which translates as "the one who brings you from darkness into light at the speed of light") through her classes, books, DVDs, and presence by teaching people how to connect to their higher consciousness through yoga, chanting, meditation and healing.

www.gurutej.com

rashida alisha hagakore
backyard bliss, poet

Rashida is a spiritual activist committed to sustaining peace through expressive arts, education & community.

hagakore@gmailcom

Faith Harrison
Breathed by Tree, illustrator

Faith Harrison is a free spirit, a dancer between worlds seeing beauty in everyday life, recreating beauty you don't see everyday.

www.FaithHarrisonArt.com

Joni James
Grandfather Tree, author and illustrator

Joni James resides in Austin, Texas, where she can still be found talking to trees.

www.AustinSocialClub@yahoo.com

Tara Khandro
Message from the Oak Tree at Uisneach, messenger

Tara Khandro loves to live a life of unfolding evolutionary heart-centric consciousness.

www.TrueHumanMedia.com

Martha Knies
Gifts from Trees: While Growing Up in Texas During the Great Depression, author

Martha Knies is a native of Marlin, Texas; Sam Houston graduate, and a retired English teacher who loves trees. Founder & president of Keep Wimberley Beautiful, she has lived in Wimberley, Texas 25 years.

Mariénne Kreitlow

poetry: *See, Maple Tree, Hoarfrost, Night Womb, Nine Inches of Rain,* and *Tree* (song on Kickstarter campaign)

Mariénne Kreitlow has been a busker, poet, playwright, and songwriter-composer who has released nine albums of original music. As "Keeper of Hearth & Home" on her fourth generation family farm in Minnesota, Mariénne's works reflect a strong sense of place and commitment to honoring the land.

www.Marienne.com

Osprey Orielle Lake

Time is Stilled in These Ancient Groves, author

Osprey Orielle Lake is the Executive Director of the Women's Earth and Climate Action Network and author of the award-winning book, *Uprisings for the Earth: Reconnecting Culture with Nature.*

www.WeCanInternational.org

Kerri Hummingbird Lawnsby

illustrations: *The Trees and Me, Observer Tree in Tasmanian Forest,* and *Miracle in the Jungle*

Kerri Hummingbird Lawnsby has been passionate about art since birth; studied art at Smith College as well as under tutelage of Grace Gibson (protegee of Hans Hofmann), and has created artwork professionally since the late 1990s.

Kerri@KerriLawnsby.com
www.KerriLawnsby.com

Steve Lingle

A Tribute to a Mighty Oak, author

Steve Lingle is a recently retired mechanic that lives in a woods with his wife, two cats and dogs.

dog.salingle@ffni.com

Thomas E. Manes

illustrations: *Sentinal Inviting* and *Tree Hugging Cactus*

Tom Manes is a landscape architect and contractor in Wimberley Texas, USA.

www.ParadiseGardenTX.com

Dianne Marion

Night Womb, illustrator

Dianne Marion is a painter and collage artist who leads art-making workshops and study groups in the Texas Hill Country, emphasizing the sacred healing that comes through self-expression.

www.SmithCreekStudios.com

Suzanne McBride

Secrets of the Trees, poet

Suzanne McBride escaped from life in corporate America as a software programmer to pursue multiple careers as a painter, sculptor, public speaker, coach and film-maker.

www.smcb.com

Hollyana Melear

Circle of Seven, author and illustrator
The Big Oak Tree, illustrator

Hollyana Melear is a working artist, teacher, and writer in Austin, Texas where she enjoys breathing in the beauty of Austin's landscapes and the hill country—which inspire paintings and joy.

www.HollyAnaMelear.com

Ann Marie Molnar

Waking Tree, poet

Ann Marie Molnar is a writer, thriving on nature, in love with trees.

eoscat@hotmail.com

Joy Pendleton
Tree of Light, author

Joy Pendleton, retired, artist, card maker, watercolor teacher.

watercolorjoy37@gmail.com

Joy Phoenix
Miracle in the Jungle, author

JOY! aka The Wish Granter, teaches how to live more joyfully and less stressfully in 3 minutes or less.

www.ExperienceJoy.com

P. Cleve Ragan
illustrations: *A Mulberry Tree: The Garden of Eden?* and *Oledas*

P. Cleve Ragan conveys her vision of life with a wide range of subject matter in a variety of genre including murals, ceramics, still life, printmaking, portraits, and figurative art.

CleveRagan@wildblue.net

Calen Rayne
untitled haiku

Rev. Dr. Calen Rayne is a Unitarian Universalist Lay Community Minister in Asheville, North Carolina.

www.RayneMaker.com

Lauren Robins
Roots Remain, author

Lauren Robins dances in gratitude for the boundless colorful joy and artistic grace that trees express.

www.LaurenRobins.com

Lillie Foley Rowden

poetry: *Lost, Reflections* and *Woodpine*

Lillie Foley Rowden, D.Min., author of *Christianity and Nature-based Spirituality*, is a spiritual mentor, retired educator and psychotherapist, who currently mentors and performs weddings and other ceremonies in the Hill Country of Texas.

lrowden@austin.rr.com

Lynne Russell

The Trees and Me, author

Lynne Russell is a semi-retired speech/language pathologist who lives in a magic forest in central Texas with her dog QT Pi.

www.cLynneRussell.com
www.LynneSlyceumOfLaughter.com

Shiila Safer, Clear Tree

stories: *Breathed by Tree* and *Soul Retrieval in the Apple Orchard*

poetry: *Breathed by Tree part two, Clear Tree, Layers, Welcome Home* and *Breathe the Wind Through Your Skin*

meditations: *Circular Breathing Practice, Listening with Your Whole Body, Being Breathed by the Tree* and *Wind in the Trees Meditation*

messages: *Words of Wisdom from Grandmother Oak, Returning, Cypress Whispers* and *Redwoods Speak*

Shiila Safer, author of *Born of the Earth: Your Journal, Poetry and Meditations in Nature*, is a nature-based coach and mentor, who assists people in returning to their deep connection with trees and the Earth, and opening to the abundant resources that are readily available through our Earth connection.

Shiila@CreativityInNature.com
www.CreativityInNature.com
www.facebook.com/secondtier.shiila

Dorey Schmidt

The Betrothal Tree, poet

Dorey Schmidt, retired professor of creative writing (University of Texas-Pan American), has written, produced and directed student plays of outdoor drama, and established troupes of senior actors. After moving to Colorado in 2012, she has launched the Autumn Actors.

Karen Smith

Gifts from the Maple Tree, poet

Karen Smith makes contemporary art quilts and writes poetry, often each inspiring the other. She loves words and challenges herself to create visual images from those that inspire her. She believes if she is still enough to listen, Grace reminds Karen of the Divine that lights her path to understanding and trust.

SophiaBlissed@gmail.com

www.gratitude-gifts.com/artcategory/KarenSmith/karen.html

Will Taegel

Preface, author

The Mulberry Tree: Garden of Eden?, author

Will Taegel is author of eight books weaving together nature, spirituality, quantum physics and psychology; most recently, *The Mother Tongue: Intimacy in the Eco-Field*. His primary focus is in assisting us in learning the language of Nature, and in returning humans to the cycle of life.

www.Earthtribe.com

www.Amazon.com/author/willtaegel

Patricia Varney, Loves Web

Loves Web, author

Patricia Varney - Sister of Trees, Lover of Earth, Reiki Master, Artist, Writer, Mental and Health Care Manager, Seeker.

pvarney14@gmail.com

Reginah WaterSpirit, Brown Dove

Lonely Child Finds Consolation with a Tree, author and illustrator

Reginah WaterSpirit is an artist and consciousness mentor using Voice Dialogue and Native American spiritual ways.

regina.waterspirit@gmail.com

Karen Wecker

Lilac's Lessons, illustrator

Karen Wecker supports herself and her cats working in front of a computer in Silicon Valley, California, and enjoys hanging out with trees in the Santa Cruz mountains and foothills.

Larry Winters, Black Peace Eagle

poetry: *She Tree, Stay* and *Come Home*

Larry Winters - Gone to war, returned from war, at war with war!

winters.lawrence@gmail.com
MakingAndUnmaking.com

Gyorge Ann Wecker Yawn

illustrations: *Roots Remain,* and *Tree School*

Gyorge Ann Wecker Yawn is the mother of six children. She has a BA in Art and Design from BYU. She worked many years in Special Education; six as a Transition Coordinator helping families transition their 3-year-olds into special ed. She loves to paint. She also teaches art to intellectually delayed young adults.

Resources

We are excited to share with you an abundance of information about trees, Mother Earth and our relationship with our living Universe. There is so much information out there—this is but a fraction of what's available, and yet, it is what's coming through the field to be shared at this time. It is heartening to connect across time and space with like-minded spirits and the current research being done in these related fields of study. Enjoy!

Suggested Reading

Abram, David. (1996). *The Spell of the Sensuous: Perception and Language in a More-Than-Human World*. New York: Vintage Books.

Abram, David. (2011). *Becoming Animal: An Earthly Cosmology*. New York: Vintage Books.

Bear Heart. (1996). *The Wind Is My Mother: The Life and Teachings of a Native American Shaman*. New York: Clarkson N. Potter Inc.

Berry, Thomas. (1988). *The Dream of the Earth*. San Francisco: Sierra Club Books.

Buhner, Stephen Harrod. (2014). *Plant Intelligence and the Imaginal Realm: Into the Dreaming of Earth*. Rochester: Bear & Company.

Chapman, Carol Flake. (2015) *Written in Water: A Memoir of Love, Death and Mystery*. Wimberley: 2nd Tier Publishing.

Cowan, Eliot. (2014). *Plant Sprit Medicine: A Journey into the Healing Wisdom of Plants*. Boulder: Sounds True Inc.

Elgin, Duane. (2009). *The Living Universe: Where Are We? Who Are We? Where Are We Going?* San Francisco: Berrett Koehler Publishers Inc.

Herman, Louis G. (2013) *Future Primal: How Our Wilderness Origins Show Us the Way Forward*. Novato: New World Library.

Kaza, Stephanie. (1993). *The Attentive Heart: Conversations with Trees*. New York: Ballentine Books.

Laszlo, Ervin. (2003). *You Can Change the World: the Global Citizen's Handbook for Living on Planet Earth*. New York: SelectBooks, Inc.

Lawlor, Robert. (1991). *Voices of the First Day: Awakening in the Aboriginal Dreamtime*. Rochester: Inner Traditions International, Ltd.

Louv, Richard. (2008). *Last Child in the Woods: Saving Our Children From Nature-Deficit Disorder*. Chapel Hill: Algonquin Books of Chapel Hill.

Mann, A.T. (2012). *The Sacred Language of Trees*. New York: Sterling Ethos.

Moon, Beth. (2014). *Ancient Trees: Portraits of Time*. New York, London: Abbeville Press Publishers.

Robbins, Jim. (2012). *The Man Who Planted Trees*. New York: Spiegel and Grau.

Safer, Shiila. (2010). *Born of the Earth: Your Journal, Poetry and Meditations in Nature*. Wimberley: 2nd Tier Publishing.

Taegel, Will. (2010). *The Sacred Council of Your Wild Heart: Nature's Hope in Earth's Crisis*. Wimberley: 2nd Tier Publishing.

Taegel, Will. (2012). *The Mother Tongue: Intimacy in the Eco-Field*. Wimberley: 2nd Tier Publishing.

Other Resources

What Plants Talk About
video.pbs.org/video/2338524490/

Music of the Plants
www.cdbaby.com/cd/damanhur

Awakening Our Relationship with Trees
youtu.be/7702KWymIT4

The Secret Life of Plants
youtu.be/sGl4btrsiHk

Do Trees Communicate?
youtu.be/iSGPNm3bFmQ

Bolivia Gives Legal Rights to the Earth
earthweareone.com/bolivia-gives-legal-rights-to-the-earth/

Ecosophy: Nature's Guide to a Better World
www.kosmosjournal.org/article/ecosophy-natures-guide-to-a-better-world/

Invocation by John Seed
www.spiritualityandpractice.com/books/excerpts.php?id=20826

Earthtribe Eco-spiritual Community
www.Earthtribe.com/

Antidepressant Microbes In Soil: How Dirt Makes You Happy
www.GardeningKnowhow.com/garden-how-to/soil-fertilizers/antidepressant-microbes-soil.htm

10 Species that Hug Trees
www.worldwildlife.org/stories/10-species-that-hug-trees

Supermind and the Primordial Avoidance by Ken Wilber
www.integrallife.com/loft-series/supermind-and-primordial-avoidance